# Miles Boyer Dechant

## AN AMERICAN IMPRESSIONIST

### 1890 - 1942

*Perkiomen Creek*, Watercolor, 1938

# MILES BOYER DECHANT

## AN AMERICAN IMPRESSIONIST

## 1890 - 1942

*by*

## DAVID MITCHELL DECHANT

Rock of Eye Press, San Diego, California

First Edition  2002


Publisher's Cataloging-in-Publication
(*Provided by Quality Books, Inc.*)


Dechant, David Mitchell.
    Miles Boyer Dechant: an American impressionist,
1890-1942 / by David Mitchell Dechant.
    p. cm.
    Includes bibliographical references.
    LCCN: 2002103254
    ISBN 0-9719124-7-5

    1. Dechant, Miles Boyer, 1890-1942. 2. Painters--
Pennsylvania--Biography. 3. Impressionism (Art)--
Pennsylvania. I. Title.

ND237.D33357D43 2002                 759.13
                                     QBI02-701384

# CONTENTS

"Art" Dechant said, "is my avocation, architecture my vocation."   Never wholly
separate, his two passions suffused and informed each other.

*Entrance to the Spring Room at Fort Zeller,*  Watercolor

# I

# "The Power of Purpose"

Miles Boyer Dechant was the consummate Sunday painter. Each weekend when he went outdoors with easel and brush, he executed his vision of the world as an American impressionist. On these endeavors the artist was armed with technical skills and aesthetic perceptions that were constantly honed in his career as an architect. Although he had only 25 years to paint, between World War I and Pearl Harbor, the total body of art he managed to produce was enormous, even working but one day a week. Close to 500 of his works survive: almost 300 watercolors, 100 etchings, and more than 100 oil paintings – all made on stolen time.

In a difficult life, Dechant found meaning and purpose in art, regardless that the recognition he received for his efforts was limited. Near the end of his life he told one son, "Most artists aren't recognized for their true capabilities and talents and accomplishments until after they're long dead, but I'd like to receive a little (recognition) before I die." He never did, and this retrospective is long overdue.

Dechant's impressionism was unique because he always incorporated architecture into the landscape. Other impressionists include architecture at times, some often, but Dechant always. In and around Berks County, Pennsylvania he painted the old buildings he loved: venerable farms, covered bridges, stone school houses and tiled barns. These buildings were constructed between 1780 and 1850 and stood undisturbed until the turn of the century. At this point they began to be taken down in wholesale fashion, and in some cases his paintings might be the only record of their existence. For this reason alone these paintings are significant. But there is the expert draftsmanship, lush color, and rock solid composition that make his paintings more than a historical record of a vanishing America. These are masterpieces of art on par with the best of the Pennsylvania Impressionist painters.

Miles' father, William Dechant, was a stern, self-made man who was romanced by the railroads early in life. When he eventually built his own house, it was alongside the railroad tracks. He never realized the heyday of the railroads had passed and that living aside of them would only bring coal dust, not prosperity. His family would sit on the porch of their new house and watch soot settle on each other.

Jumping back in time to 1805, Europeans from all countries were immigrating to America by the thousands, seeking better lives regardless that the United States of America was a 29-year-old country still struggling to maintain its union and legitimacy abroad. In Kreuznach, Germany, Jacob Dechant (Miles Dechant's great grandfather) then 22 years old was among those packing their belongings for the trip to the New World. Traveling alone he crossed the Atlantic Ocean on a crowded "sail vessel" which landed in Philadelphia. He continued on to Baltimore, Maryland to commence "his preparatory training for the holy ministry." He was ordained in 1808 and married the same year to Rebecca Andre. Rev. Jacob and his family lived the typical lives of poor itinerant ministers in America. In the course of having 12 children, he preached his way through Pennsylvania and eventually reached the "Far West" of Ohio.

Along this circuitous route, Jacob Dechant worked with the German-speaking immigrants of his homeland. Life on the frontier was difficult, and he gradually headed his large family back East, towards civilization. He took charge of his last ministry in the Oley Valley, incredibly rich farmland, just east of Reading, Pennsylvania. This was the Oley Valley whose scenes were painted so lovingly a century later by Miles, his great grandson.

Oley had been settled by the French Huguenots, but it was a melting pot of French, Irish, and German people as was most of Pennsylvania. He was to spend 13 years there before Asiatic cholera struck him on the way back from a Synod meeting in Maryland. He died at age 48 leaving his widow and 10 remaining children. In time three of those would become ministers in the Evangelical Reformed Church, causing the church biographer to write, "Truly, he founded a Levitical family!"

The oldest of Jacob's sons was the Rev. Frederick Dechant, Miles' grandfather. In family photos Frederick appears stern and rather grim. His bearing in speech, outlook, and demeanor was described as

"Germanic." He gave his four children a strict religious upbringing, instilling a strong work ethic. His oldest son William (who would become Miles' father) had a personality cut from the same cloth. In fact, their personalities were so perfectly matched (idiosyncratically) they found each other intolerable. William was determined to not become a fourth Reverend Dechant, and so he left school and home when he was in the eighth grade.

This independent young man struck out from his home to become a railroad man. Even as a boy, William had seen that fortunes were made from the railroads. He was eager to make his own fortune, and sought to be free of his father. What William got was the lowliest job the railroads had to offer, a telegraph operator's job, reading short notes and tapping out the keys. The only advantage to this situation was the lull time between messages, giving him time to study engineering books. He saw this as the route to furthering himself in the railroad's employ. He was very diligent in his studies, and in time essentially taught himself engineering.

In 1885 the serious, self-taught civil engineer married Rebecca Hagman of Philadelphia. As they began married life William held a variety of engineering jobs throughout Pennsylvania including roadmaster of the Philadelphia & Reading Railroad and division engineership on the Mahanoy Division Railroad in the coal fields in Pennsylvania.

Out of the blue William was offered the opportunity to head an existing engineering firm in Reading with the possibility of eventual ownership. Somewhat reluctantly he left the railroads. Five years later he succeeded the owner of Kendall Bros. and renamed the firm for himself. In his own words and with typical understatement he wrote in a 1925 resume: "After I became the owner of the business, with efficient assistants, I personally undertook some contract construction." That

Miles' mother, Rebecca Hagman Dechant, was a jolly person with a great sense of humor. Miles' affectionate etching (below), done in 1933, shows the effects of age, senility and arthritis on his mother. Even impaired, she could enjoy a good laugh.

"contract construction" to which he referred would ultimately include a gravity railroad, two hydroelectric power plants, the establishment of several water companies, and numerous commercial buildings and public projects all in and around Reading.

As the 19th century drew to a close, Reading was still a vibrant railroad city. Period photographs depict the classic scenes of optimistic Americana: May Day parades, new churches, and swimsuit contests. Observed from the Berks County Fair's hot air balloon, Reading would have appeared to be a city inside the top of a giant volcano whose vortex mixed row houses with business buildings, churches, restaurants, and factories. The whole that industrialization had to offer was within easy walking distance, and the railroads provided this volcano's belching smoke. Like lava flowing down the sides, railroad tracks radiated out of Central Station to link Reading with Philadelphia 60 miles southeast and New York 100 miles to the northeast. The encircling hills formed the volcano's rim where a huge, full-blown Japanese pagoda would, within a few years, tower just above the suburb of Mt. Penn. The pagoda, an out-of-place oddity, would hint that Reading had a quirky artistic side as well.

So it was into this bustling industrial milieu that Miles was born on January 10, 1890. In early childhood Miles' hazel eyes were forever fixed on his older brother Frederick. Three years younger, little Miles struggled to keep up in every way. When Fred played with his friends, Miles would follow the older boys around, always trying to join in the fun. He kept saying "me too, me too" which led Fred to give him the affectionate nickname of "Little Metoo." This was a harbinger of the relationship they were to have for life. Fred would always remain the clearly dominant brother. They had two younger sisters, Mary and Sarah.

Just as birth order puts parameters on all lives, elementary school also imposed its own set of restrictions on young Miles. He was born a natural left-hander, but the rule of the day was "write on the right." School

Miles Dechant, far left, at age 10. "His artistic inclinations," Miles later wrote about himself, "showed themselves very early and as young as 8 years old, he copied (from lithographs) birds and flowers." To the right are his siblings, Mary 7, Sarah 1, Fred 12.

was inflexible; anyone caught writing left-handed would have his knuckles rapped with the ruler. After the teacher's long black dress swept by Miles' desk, he would quickly switch back to his left hand and sketch in the margins of his schoolbooks. By this "rule" he became ambidextrous: a right-handed writer and a left-handed artist.

When Miles was 11-years-old, the family took a trip to Buffalo, New York to visit the Pan-American Exposition. It was a huge spectacle, the largest he had ever seen. His father, a staunch Republican, stood with his sons in a long line to shake President McKinley's hand. No sooner had Miles grasped McKinley's hand than guards pushed the line along "as logs are propelled down a sluice." Walking away from the tent, still giddy with 11-year-old enthusiasm, Miles heard shots. Police ran through the hysterical crowds, and the Dechant family came to the realization that President McKinley had just been shot. Miles had been among the last people to shake the assassinated President's hand.

The family left for home immediately afterward, not knowing the President's fate. Miles read the newspaper daily for news about

McKinley, and when he died eight days later it came as a blow to the nation and especially to a sensitive boy. Miles had become not only a witness to history, but to life's brevity. Even years later, he would describe this as one of the important events in his life.

With less of his childhood innocence intact, Miles went on to the new Reading Boys' High School for his freshman year in 1906, the same year it opened. Although it was a public school (and for boys only), it had a demanding curriculum. This was a preparatory school environment akin to Andover. The school principal "expected the boys to be self-starters and work things out, rather than wait for handouts from their elders." Miles' family had equally high expectations for him; brother Fred had set the bar still higher, earning excellent grades. Miles was equal to the challenge, being very driven and very serious. The down side was that he developed a tendency to worry about things at which he excelled.

He developed a habit of sitting very still and letting his eyes glaze as if in a dream state, but his outward calmness belied the maelstrom of activity inside his head. When Miles entered into his private world of intense thought, worry became overwhelming. He worried about classes and test results as if they were a life and death struggle. By his junior year Miles had pushed himself into a state of mental and physical exhaustion resulting in a nervous breakdown.

Today "nervous breakdown" is more narrowly defined as depression, anxiety disorder, hallucination, or other conditions. In 1908 one diagnosis covered a large map, and Miles' position on it remains a mystery. What is known about his last two years in high school also creates a puzzling picture. He was not graduated from Boys' High until he was 20-years-old, yet he was one of the class orators. There is speculation that he may have taken a year off, or maybe he devoted himself to manual arts classes for a time as part of the school's "project method."

To support the latter theory are two beautifully made tall clock cases that Miles completed in his senior year. Each clock represents month

One of two Chippendale style tall clock cases Dechant made in high school woodshop. He sold the first case to pay for the clock movement of the second case, which he kept.

upon month of work, and it is doubtful whether the pair could have been completed within the demands of a full curriculum. These cases are the first extant examples of his artistry. Although not original in design, they exhibit the skills of a natural born craftsman. In spite of having fairly primitive work tools, the results are refined and perfect. He told his sons that the most difficult part was getting the glue joints tight. He used horse-hoof glue and learned that glue on a cold joint would not set up right. His answer was to heat the boards near a radiator and get them close to glue temperature before closing the joinery. The difficulty of executing these antiquated working methods underscores the artistic achievement represented in the clock cases.

Woodworking requires intense concentration, for without this either the workmanship will become rough; or worse, one can be badly injured by the tools. The focus woodworking required seems to have been a good match for Miles' personality, diverting his thoughts from worry and toward the dangers of the spinning saw blade. If this was the cure, it seems to have worked. By the time he finished high school, his mental health was a non-issue.

The title of his high school oration was "The Power of Purpose" and its five-page script addressed several themes. One foretold so much of his own life that it stands out from the body of the speech almost as a biblical prophecy:

> We are all creatures of choice...the course of our lives largely follows the direction we give them in our youth. Two courses lie open to us; the one bending our energies to be able to help others in noble self-sacrifices and in a sturdy adherence to the cause of right and truth, the other a sordid one of gain and money for self-gratification regardless of principle and right. Ourselves, our homes, our community, and our country will be benefited by the former course, disgraced and degraded by the latter.

He reworks the same theme later in the speech, and more explicitly lays out the role of the artist:

Our aim should be, not to get a living primarily, but to perform well a certain work. A man should not be hired who does work simply for the money, but one should be selected who does it for the love of it. Grave and honest men do not work for gold. They work for love, for honor, for character. When Michelangelo was commanded by the Pope to undertake the work at St. Peter's, he consented only upon the condition that he should receive no salary, but that he should labor for the love of God alone.

He believed in the words of his altruistic high school speech and contemplated the artist's path. He wrote, "I would like to have followed an artistic career as a pure artist, but I was discouraged by my father and uncle, and I decided to study architecture and make that my life's work." Following that course, he applied to the University of Pennsylvania. The application process then was far more streamlined: upon paperwork completion, admission became automatic. Miles left home for Philadelphia and the University of Pennsylvania in the fall of 1910.

Just as in high school, he was an intense student. Always striving for perfection, Dechant fell into the habit of working all night in the architectural department. He would work until he was in a state of physical collapse, at which point he would push drafting tables together and get a few hours sleep. His fellow students caught on to his routine and played a prank on him. Shortly before class, as he lay sleeping, a group of friends held him down and shaved off half his moustache. There was

Miles at work in the Department of Architecture at the University of Pennsylvania. One evening he carved his initials into the wood casement around these windows. His graffiti remained for many years.

no time to go home and shave completely, so he spent the school day half complete. Miles took it with his characteristic good humor.

With or without a moustache, his first two years of architecture school were devoted to the basics: descriptive geometry, elements of architecture, shade, shadow, and perspective. He was outstanding in these as well as his prerequisites: math, chemistry, English literature, and French. The university graded numerically then, and when Miles received a 99 in one class, he went directly to the professor and demanded, "Why a 99? I got every question right. I did everything right!" Calmly the professor replied, "Miles, I gave you a 99 because nobody is perfect."

His professor was probably correct, but the student could not see it. He demanded perfection from himself, no matter that it left him stressed and exhausted. The circumstances that had led to his earlier mental health problems were starting to repeat. Miles' world was rapidly closing in on him, and he did not realize it. He continued working with a fury bent on self-destruction. He had his second nervous breakdown during finals in spring 1912.

In the words of the university newspaper: "Dechant had to leave the university because of exhaustion brought about by overwork." Agitated, defeated and physically ill, he returned home to Reading. As his family picked him up at the train station, their concern can be imagined: this was his second nervous breakdown in three years. Was Miles to have permanent melancholia?

Miles was turned over to the family physician for treatment, and the doctor prescribed a novel cure. He advised: "...Miles needs to have a rowboat, and row up and down the Schuylkill River every day. Rain or shine, no matter what, just get out and row. Row for at least five miles every day."

The prescription was followed. His father bought him a small rowboat, and he learned how to propel it. Miles had bypassed adolescence without rebellion and now very quietly, through his rowing, he was going to confront it. Like a post-adolescent Huck Finn, he began navigating through the meandering river on his own. The river was an important metaphor for Mark Twain, and so it was also for Miles Dechant. The river taught him to take control of his own boat and to set his own course outside the limitation of parents, school, and older brother.

Off the river, Miles continued to chart his own recovery through art work, just as in high school. Woodworking as a therapy was swapped for drawing. He sketched castles and maidens at a small desk in his third story attic bedroom. Drawing allowed him diversion from the trance of concentration that inexplicably held him. This was his road away from worry and introspection. It was far safer for him to channel his thoughts toward a noble purpose – art.

He kept at this regimen throughout the four seasons. A year is a long time to spend in recovery by rowing and drawing. It cured not only his mental condition but also transformed and tempered his artistic spirit. He had always had the hands of an artist, for he was a born draftsman. But he needed this time to develop his soul as well. On the river he formed impressions that would last a lifetime: sunlight glinting off rocks worn smooth, the way mist hangs on the distant horizon, the feeling of water on his sunburned hands, and the color of the day.

In the process of developing a more independent sense of self and an identity as an artist, Miles had recovered his mental health. By fall 1913, he was ready to put his year on the river behind him and return to the university. However, his parents were reluctant to see him resume school, and they put some precautions in place in hopes of preventing another relapse. First, Miles' living conditions were to be changed: he would live at the house of his mother's brother in Philadelphia. Second, sister Mary was to accompany him as a chaperone de facto. This suited Mary very well as she had been petitioning their father to allow her to attend the Pennsylvania Museum and School of Industrial Art in Philadelphia. The father, who had originally stood in complete opposition to Mary, allowed her to register. Uncle

When his sister, Mary, attended the Pennsylvania Museum and School of Industrial Art, she painted this small design and put her initials on it, M.A.D., Mary Angeline Dechant. Many years later it became the design for a commercial playing-card package without her consent and she was upset when, to get a deck, she had to pay for it.

Mary Dechant: *Muse*, Gouache, 1914

Joe Hagman was to keep a stern and watchful eye on Miles and Mary. That was the plan.

Uncle Joe was the perfect picture of respectability. A successful and charismatic executive with the Baldwin locomotive works, he had a wife and one daughter. He was to provide moral guidance for his niece and help his nephew recuperate, and that is where the plan went astray. Uncle Joe was an agreeable but lax guardian, and moral guidance was not his province. He was a jolly, nearsighted man, and his giant "corporation" would shake in rolls of laughter at a good practical joke. In short he was something of a rascal ⁓ and a maid chaser as well. They loved Uncle Joe, but his legacy to them was dubious: he introduced them to smoking.

As an artistic affectation pipe smoking was nonpareil, and Miles acquired the habit that would last his lifetime. When father William found that his children were smoking, and he did find out, he was more than displeased. He propositioned Miles with the words "…it's bad for your health, and I'll tell you what I'm going to do. If you stop and promise never to smoke again, I'll give you $100." This was a handsome sum at the time, and Miles turned it down. He was not ready to lose his new found pastime, and he pacified his father by downplaying its importance. "Smoking," he said, "is the only bad habit I have, and a corncob pipe at that."

Despite smoking, Miles was not cavalier about his health. He took steps to safeguard his mind from his almost involuntary whole body immersion into studies. Incapable of casual and relaxed study, he knew he needed to achieve some balance in his life. He joined the architects' rowing team in his junior year, and he also participated as an assistant scene painter in the play presented by the Architectural Society. Most important ⁓ he studied art. Miles took classes given by Professor G. W. Dawson whose tonalist style was delicate and poetic. Adopting this, Miles bathed his student paintings in a monochromatic but golden light. The harmony he achieved in these paintings paralleled the harmony he finally seemed able to achieve in life.

A golden watercolor painted during his senior year.

*The Old Mill*, Watercolor, 1914

This more balanced approach carried over into Miles' senior year as honor after honor found him. He was voted into the Architectural Society, a fraternal organization that represented the crème de la crème of the university's architects. He won the gold medal for having the highest total average for architectural design for four years. Concurrent with his course of study he accepted the extracurricular project of designing a large estate. The student architect called it *A Country Hermitage*, and it sat on 80 acres of rolling oak and pine in Cumru Township. *(Opposite)* On a final note, he was promoted to master scene painter for the architectural school's year end play, "The Blue Smock." In high spirits, Miles Dechant left the university and entered the real world, one at war.

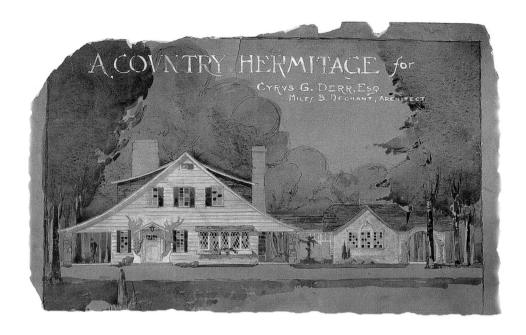

Just two weeks before his graduation in 1915, a German U-boat had sunk the passenger ship Lusitania, killing 1,198 people. President Woodrow Wilson vowed that the United States would remain neutral, but the question was for how long? Under this dark cloud, Dechant set about beginning his career as an architect. As did all architects he would first have to serve an apprenticeship, and he was hired by a large Philadelphia firm, Mellor and Meigs, as an architectural draftsman. It was a long drop from superstar student to lowly draftsman in a big architectural office.

In his spare time he had set his sights on the Roman Prize, a design contest open to any architect in the country under 30 years of age. The winner would receive $3,000 and a three-year course of study in Rome. This was the most prestigious young architectural competition in the United States at the time. Miles was one of four finalists in the nation, and he had high hopes of winning the trip to Europe, even though the continent was in complete turmoil. As if he were blind to this, Miles devoted his free time to the final leg of the Roman Prize competition.

But the traditional annual family summer vacation threatened to derail his plans. The Dechants' custom was to spend the last month of summer at Mt. Gretna in the Pennsylvania mountains where the higher altitude provided a break from the summer heat in the days before air conditioning. Miles loved being with his family in the relaxed resort atmosphere, and it was a hard offer to refuse. He decided to spare two days over a weekend, little knowing that this would turn into a life changing event. Before he arrived, the family had set up camp and become friendly with a family from Lancaster named Garvin. They enjoyed attending outdoor theater and dining together and scheduled their activities to coincide. James R. Garvin, the father, was younger than William Dechant by almost 20 years, but otherwise the families were comparable. They had children of similar ages, even names ‒ both families had a daughter named Sarah. Miles Dechant was introduced to Sarah Garvin during this weekend trip.

He rendered the resort at Mt. Gretna using little puddles of paint, which as they dried, pulled their most intense colors to the edges, like the rings around Saturn.

*Mt. Gretna,* Watercolor, 1914

Sarah Garvin was 23 and the first female mathematics teacher at an all-boys high school. She was graduated from Millersville Normal School (now Millersville University of Pennsylvania) when she was only 19. The college yearbook described her as being "Divinely tall, and most divinely fair." Indeed she was tall for the day, looking eye to eye with Miles who never stood more than 5 feet 8 inches, on a tall day. They had much in common: they were both serious, conscientious people; both had been class orators. They were united and motivated by a belief in God. The attraction that began was built from shared values, and besides, Miles was smitten with her.

SARAH L. GARVIN, ................Lancaster, Pa.
Board of Editors—Page.
"Divinely tall, and most divinely fair."

This tall, stately girl is one of the Lancaster girls in room nine. She is one of our bright, studious girls who, besides mastering her lessons, manages to have a good time socially. Sarah is one of our chief snappers and is often seen over at the store talking to Bill. Since Sarah's father is a treasurer this may account for her fondness for "Bills." Sarah has a mania for collecting odd admirers. Paul and the "Dago" are two of her chief admirers. Lately she seems to be very much interested in Baltimore and a young man residing there. She is an excellent reciter and is an active member of Page Society. She is always calm and collected, and does not allow her temper to become ruffled in any way.

*Touchstone 1912 Annual.* Sarah's peers also voted her "most versatile."

Sarah was still living at her parents' home in Lancaster and Miles in Philadelphia. The distance that separated them, as covered in a Model T Ford, led them to believe they had discovered every road pothole in Pennsylvania. Consequently they wrote each other notes more often than they met. As pen pals, they gradually built and strengthened their relationship.

The United States' pledge of neutrality in the European war was unraveling. In the beginning of 1917 Germany announced unrestricted submarine warfare on the Atlantic Ocean, and America responded by breaking off diplomatic relations. Germany then sank six American vessels. It appeared as if Germany, confident of victory, was openly challenging the United States to declare war.

On a rainy day in April 1917, Miles opened the newspaper and saw the headline: President Wilson Asks for War! Wilson portrayed the fight as America's noble duty, "The present German submarine warfare is a warfare against mankind...It is a war against all nations, the challenge is to all mankind...The world must be made safe for democracy." Both Dechant and the nation were stirred by these words, but neither went to enlist.

Despite the patriotic fervor sweeping the nation, so few men were enlisting in military service that the Selective Service Act was called upon. All men between the ages of 21 and 30 were to register for war service at their regular voting places on June 5, 1917. To do this Miles returned to Reading where local Socialists carried signs reading: "If this is a popular war, why conscription?" He ignored the signs and registered. On that one day some 9,500,000 other Americans did the same.

Miles had been assigned a draft number between 1 and 10,500, and if that number did not come up he could stay home. In Washington, D.C. the numbered black capsules were placed in a glass bowl to be drawn by blindfolded officials. Each time a number was drawn, it would be flashed to all the local draft boards to check their lists.

On the morning of July 20, Secretary of War Baker put his hand into the bowl and drew the first number, 258. Miles recalled feeling his heart skip a beat as he read his evening paper. His number had not been pulled, but he hated living with uncertainty as if his life were a lottery. Overnight the uncertainty weighed on him, and by morning he developed a course of action. He composed a letter to remove himself from these tenterhooks: "I hereby apply for enlistment in the Ordnance Enlisted Reserve Corps...," and he mailed it off on July 21, 1917.

Graduation photo of Miles Boyer Dechant from the University
of Pennsylvania, age 25.

One last photo in front of his parents' home, and he
was off to Army basic training. August 1, 1917

# II

# The Great War

The United States Army wasted no time welcoming its new recruit into the Ordnance Corps. Less than a week after he applied to enlist, Miles was in basic training camp at Frankfort Arsenal in Pennsylvania. Now that he was in the Army, the interminable uncertainties of the last two years were over. No longer waiting for the other shoe to drop, he cast his fate "into the hands of God." As he said goodbye to his family and friends, he did his best to assure them he would be fine. He wrote from camp on his second day with a bit of embellishment: "I have by this time become quite accustomed to Army life, and it seems to be agreeing with me as I am well and happy…The idea of going to France soon appeals intensely to me, and tell father not to interfere with this idea."

Two months later he was assigned to the 42nd Rainbow Division and moved to its staging area, Camp Mills, Long Island, New York. "You ought to see this camp," he wrote, "it is a marvel. Everywhere you look, you see gray lines of regiments, with bayonet-headed rifles, marching in dusty lines along the flat of the horizon. Glancing backward, you see tent, and tent, and then more tents." Although his letters home were always cheerful and reassuring in tone, one senses between the lines that the first months of Army life were falling short of his expectations. "Loafing jobs" and the slow pace often bored him. He was also disappointed that the Army didn't provide quality provisions for the men. He learned that, for good boots, or sweaters, or sleeping bags, it was necessary to write the folks back home.

He had momentary enthusiasms, though:

> Today Uncle Sam made us a present of a fine automatic .45 Colt pistol, which are commonly known as 'gats' among the fellows. They are a savage looking weapon. How proud I feel to carry this manly weapon at my side. Tomorrow we receive instruction in the taking care of this weapon. No doubt but we will receive instruction in firing the pistols in France or wherever we are. Please do not tell Aunt Tishie that I carry one of these instruments. If you do, tell her it isn't loaded.

A few days later, his enthusiasm for his pistol passed:

> …and it makes me shiver in my shoes to even take the magazines out of their case on my belt. I hope I shall never be forced to use the weapon on a German brother.

He was conflicted not only about his sidearm, but also about his place and function within the Army.

Three months of training had done little to clear up his confusion. Prepared or not, he made ready to leave and was allowed one last visit with his family. As he kissed his mother, and shook his father's hand good-bye, he tried to put on his best possible face.

> Departure yesterday was hard for me to bear. I only gave vent to my emotions when in bed last evening. There were many weeping mothers at camp yesterday afternoon when I came back, and it sent a chill of homesickness over me. As I look over the beautiful fields with stacks of corn and the trees twinning those lovely colors, I think of how I enjoyed these things at home around this time of the year. I must try now to forget being a pessimist, and look forward to the time of coming home again. You have no idea how one feels, when he thinks he shall probably never return and see home. But I am going to come back and will look forward with all my heart and soul to that time.

"Bon voyage," his parents' cablegram read. Miles left New York Harbor headed for Europe on a troopship. On that memorable day "when I was

Ready to leave.

Miles (far left) two days before departure. October 16, 1917

in the hold of the ship, I offered up a prayer and gave my life in the hands of God. It was truly a red-letter day in my life." His ship traveled through the "most dangerous sector of the war zone." He was under orders to sleep with his life vest on because the threat of torpedoes was so great. This was certainly not the trip to Europe he had envisioned when seeking the Roman Prize in architecture, but when he sighted France the war was almost forgotten.

From the moment he arrived in St. Nazaire, he saw only the France of his imagination:

> You have known how interested I have always been in the possibility of seeing France sometime in my life, and how in my spare moments I would dream of those beautiful architectural monuments of which I studied. My wishes have come true, and as I looked upon this beautiful and humble domestic architecture of the peasants, my ideals as an artist were realized. I have made many mental notes and besides a number of quick pencil sketches.

Inspired as he was by his glorious vision of France, he wanted to do his part in its liberation:

> Think of these poor French people who have given all their children.

There comes a time in one's life when we must sacrifice ourselves for the advancement of civilization and a noble cause…

With "…nothing to do at the depot," Miles was certain his talents were being wasted and that as a "lowly corporal," he was doing nothing to help bring down the Kaiser. "What the Sam Hill is the use in sitting in an office all through the war?" he wondered, and wrote his parents for advice:

> You know I would like to advance as much as possible while in the Army. I want to be in the work I am most fitted for, and if I stay here in the Ordnance simply tracing drawing after drawing, I don't see much chance for advancement. I am not a mechanical engineer, and yet here I am in that department, not knowing beans where I stand. If however I were in the Camouflage Corps, my services would be much more to the advantage of both the government and myself. I am going to ask you what you think of my trying to get transferred to the Camouflage Corps. You know what I like to do is designing and construction, and no doubt in the Camouflage there would be a good chance for advancement. Moreover I don't know but what there would be a likely chance of landing a commission.

His father replied in a telegram: "Our present advice, stay where you are." He ignored the advice, but remained bureaucratically ensnared with the Ordnance department at Nevers. Still chaffing, he accidentally gained the ear of someone who could help:

> One day I was showing (a sketch) to several interested fellows, when Major Rice walked up and said in a pleasant tone, 'What is the matter with that?' One could see by the expression on his face that he was awfully pleased, and he called me into his office, and from that time on has taken such a keen interest in whatever I do. I have been doing drafting and working along my own lines. I never dreamt of ever doing this in the army. He gave me orders to go downtown, and purchase for him a full set of pastel colors. He is an artist himself and is a connoisseur of paintings.

The day after this happened he gave me special work along my own lines at the depot, and I had quite a little drawing room all my own fixed up. The following Sunday Major Rice relieved me from duty, and said 'Now you go out sketching and show me what you did in the evening.' Now this is a major's point of view. Major Rice said it was a pity to have a man who, as he said, is so interested in architecture, not to have a chance to benefit by this wonderful country, overflowing in every nook and corner with works of art. I have made in all about 9 sketches, some of which I gave to the major who was very much pleased with them.

Dechant mailed some of his artwork back home as the war waged on. "I made this (picture frame) in the evenings between letter (writing) days, and the whole thing I carved with my good friend, the pen knife. The wood is from an old gun stock and will be a remembrance of this war." The painting inside the frame was painted later and based on a French sketch.

*Frame*, Walnut, 1918
*French Chateau*, Oil, 1921

Dechant's much improved situation lasted about two weeks.

My ambition of gradually growing, and advancing in the work under Major Rice suddenly took a turn one day, when he said he was going to lose me. You don't know how badly I felt, and he expressed his thoughts as being sorry to see me go. He had gotten word from headquarters; to send me there.

Disappointed but determined to remain cheerful, he closed with "Spring is coming and I don't care then whether they send me to China, Ha!" He set out across France in the bleakness of a February landscape toward new adventures. "As you will notice by my new address, I am advancing. Ha! That is going up closer to the action as it were." His new station was Is-sur-Tille, a village near Dijon on the eastern side of France. He wrote home, "…(my new depot) is a great place and we are quartered in a most picturesque place." After the war ended, he wrote his parents a much more accurate account of his first days at his new station:

> We landed at Is-sur-Tille on a very bad rainy day, one of those typical French dismal days. Then we marched about 2 miles to where we were to be quartered, and it sure was some quarters. There was an old barn, open hay shed and a ramshackle looking frame structure. After looking around I decided that the old haymow was the best place, so I took my humble abode in the hay amid numerous rats and all sorts of vermin. In the courtyard of the old billet there was a manure pile and around it was about two feet of water and mud, which we fellows had to stand in at mess time. We always had to chase the chickens off from the dining room table before we sat down on nice wet planks. Then, if it was raining real hard, which most of the time it was, we could look for the canvas roof to cave in at any time due to the surplus of water on it. Many times I have eaten my meal consisting of corn beef hash out in the open and raining torrents so that the hash looked more like stew than anything else. But those days were great days when men forgot about these hardships and put their strength into the one great aim of winning the war. Long columns of boys were seen in the morning when it was not yet light bearing not the implements of war, but of labor. Their stern faces bore the smile and radiance of good cheer yet, in their expressions could be traced that longing for the day when they could raise their hats in cheers for their coming victory. They were living for that day when, turning to go home, they would say to heroic France, 'We have saved you.'

Dechant settled into a busy life at Is-sur-Tille, and gradually ceased mentioning his attempts at a commission. He briefly resigned himself to his initiation in ordnance work. With pick and shovel, he helped construct enormous steel warehouses for the munitions of war. He heaved heavy boxes of ammunition and supplies onto trucks and trains, and then delivered them to forward divisions. One night in late May he received orders to go with an Irish corporal, his own age, to convey munitions to a gap in the French line on the road between Chateau-Thierry and Paris. While underway, an artillery raid caught the convoy. This was the first time he felt the shock and saw the flash of bursting shells. Although he had a revolver strapped to his belt, it was useless. His life truly was in the hands of God with the war bearing down upon him so closely. He experienced two more shellings on three successive nights, while he supplied the battle of Chateau-Thierry, sweeping through street after street. In the town buildings fell as shells hit them from heavy guns. Machine guns rattled from doorways and street corners, but the munitions were delivered every night. Of the 8,000 Americans involved in this battle, 1,600 were killed and 2,513 wounded. This battle, General Pershing said, "stopped the German advance on Paris."

The bombardments he lived through shook him from his very brief complacency as an ordnance man. Although Dechant had done his part, he felt he should be doing more:

> It worries me at times to really know whether I should be fighting, or this work. I feel all the time as if I ought to actually fight, and help in this way. I am doing my work as best I know how, and there has to be someone to do this. It is a hard matter to decide. It is also harder to transfer to another branch of the service. I have learned a great deal about artillery in my work, and I would like getting into the artillery.

While Dechant remained conflicted about his place within the Army, he also remained in Is-sur-Tille, doing the exact same job. By coincidence, he found himself living next door to the YMCA hut at Is-sur-Tille. From training camp on, the YMCA had been a presence "making everything as comfortable as possible for the soldiers." The canteen sold fruit and candy, and freely dispensed YMCA logo writing paper. The Y also boosted morale with talks given for the benefit of the American soldiers. He described one such evening:

> …there was a song service held. We sang such songs as 'Old Black Joe,' 'The Little Gray Home in the West,' etc. After the address delivered by a Methodist minister, we had movies. The movie was entitled 'The Marriage of Molly-O.' It is great to go to these Sunday evening meetings. Half of the service is purely religious and half secular I should say.

For Sunday church services he began branching out from the YMCA, seeking local churches. The attraction was definitely not the services, which were Catholic and in French. Rather, he was inspired by the ecclesiastical architecture of small quaint churches as well as magnificent cathedrals. Of the former he observed,

> I found the service interesting although I did not understand all the sermon. The church was in every respect a simple and dignified structure expressing in its ensemble the traits and characteristics of the ancient Frenchmen who built it. It is, in its crudeness, that one finds the expression of individuality and beauty. Nothing modern could boast of an aesthetic character as is expressed here. The little enrichment found in the decorative detail bore in some places marks of despondency, as it seemed to me. Here the chisel slipped in the carver's hand and at some places the lines were lost and at others they would burst anew into lovely and luxuriant expression. All this shows the sentiments of the workman and in its hidden beauty lies buried the soul and spirit of the hands who did it. Here again the tower was a marked feature of the building and the main entrance was through the tower. The walls of the tower were old and crumbling, and moss and wild flowers grew in the chinks of mortar joints. But what were most inspiring were the old timbers that formed the lintel of the doorway. These old timbers were also worn and wearing out, but like sincere and venerable folks who work until the end, they were still doing their duty and holding up the heavy weight of the superstructure.

"I talk so much about these old churches that probably you get tired of it," he apologized. But he didn't stop, and saved his most vivid writing for the most poetic of all the churches, the great cathedrals of France:

What glory, and stupendous thought were expressed in this noble edifice reared for the purpose of worshiping God. As I approached this building, its massive towers rising to a great height, and from which the chimes were softly pealing with music as I have never heard before in chimes; I could not help but feel the insignificance of man alongside this mass of stone, and I felt the thrill of ages, as I gazed and wondered at the statuettes now broken and crumbling to powder. I stood for a long time looking into its past history, for I could readily tell the time in which it was built from its decorative detail and proportions of the fenestration. But my heart leaped for joy as I stepped onto the threshold of the door.

When I entered this cathedral, the choir was chanting an anthem. The little boys dressed in their white garbs looked up as they sang, and truly it was a glorious picture. The high priest dressed in beautifully embroidered garments stood at the altar with his back turned towards the people, and held above his head a pot of incense before the gilded crucifix. I saw the French soldiers in the church kneeling at prayer. I heard the loud appeal for victory in the Great War and then in the quietness of all, as the organ stopped playing I heard the chimes ring in the great and lofty tower. A tower which has borne those chimes for ages, and when they struck, the very walls of the church seemed to shake and vibrate. Amid the crowds of people who were leaving the church, I stood and remained, until I was alone and then as I walked up and down the long aisles looking and admiring the beautiful pieces of statuary my thoughts vanished into the middle ages. I tramped on the warm tile floor where hundreds and thousands of sainted monks had walked. I felt and leaned against the marble columns that supported those gorgeous vaults of gothic tracery. I remained, and saw the last ray of sun shining through the rose window over the altar, and as the bells tolled 6:00 o'clock I left and probably shall never see it again. I shall not be remembered there, but the glorious church is imprinted on my vision, as something not to be forgotten.

More than remember the churches of France, Dechant refined his own ambition to "some day build or design a church, providing I live through this war." His father responded to this news with his own: their church in Reading had proposed new construction. Trapped in France, Miles jokingly replied, "Can't you postpone it? Ha!" He then counseled, "Get a good architect and look to its aesthetic value as well as to its practical necessities. A church should speak for itself, it should be a glorious building, one that hears the spirit of sacredness; and one that even sings of the men's hearts and souls that built it."

His own heart longed to be home, building that church. The longing went deeper than his own artistic ambitions; a large part of soldier Dechant was just plain homesick. "I have been wondering about all at home the last few days and especially more today. I sometimes get one of these spells of homesickness, but then I start to whistle and sing that song 'Pack up your troubles in your old kit bag and smile, smile, smile.'" These few sentences characterize pages of his letters home: he would mention glimpses into what he might be feeling or experiencing, and then cover his true emotions with songs, poetry, church descriptions, or anything else. He attempted, as much he possibly could, to insulate his family from worry. He constantly reassured them that he had a "tremendous appetite" and was happy.

Pen pal Sarah Garvin

On account of homesickness, Dechant loved receiving mail. He admonished all those he wrote: please write back! His favorite correspondent was Sarah Garvin. Their long distance courtship was twinned from letters answered on a five-week delay. Sarah sent him not one, but three Christmas boxes, and she knitted him a muffler. That put Miles in a quandary. "I have two mufflers now," he wrote his parents. "Did I tell you Sarah Garvin knitted me one? Should I give the one Emily Strauss made me to some poor fellow who hasn't any? Please don't tell Emily." Emily's muffler didn't stand a chance.

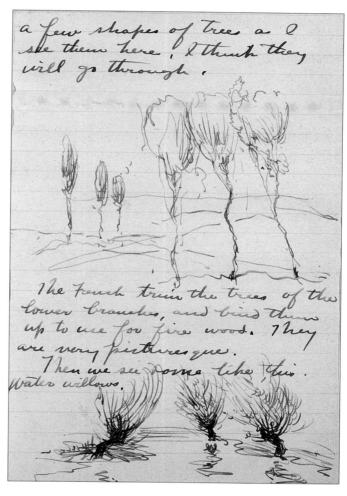

Dechant sometimes drew little sketches in his letters home. His second sentence, "I think they will go through," refers to the Army censor. Because of censorship, he couldn't reveal his location, or activities, which forced him to write more about his artistic feelings.

Even though Miles was far, far from home, he was faithful to his pen pal. Writing Uncle Joe he said, "You probably wonder how I like French girls. Well they are all very fine & nice, but By Jove they don't come up to our girls in the States, especially the one in Lancaster." Sarah reciprocated his feelings and in support of his absence even applied at the War Department. She was hired in August, and began preparing statistical data for the Funding Division of the Army's Ordnance Branch. Though Miles and Sarah were far apart, they were now attached – to the same branch of the Army.

As Sarah acclimated herself to civilian Army work, Miles started to carve out his own niche within the regular Army.

> The officers began to recognize in different men their particular abilities along different lines and, as mine was drafting or, rather, as I became known as the draftsman at Nevers, I was given this sort of work. I made illustrative drawings complete of the breech mechanism of the 155mm French Howitzer, a gun that was greatly used in this war. One of my officers gave me a place to work in a frame shack, and I had to build my own drawing table, drawing board, and T square. Then it was discovered that I could paint signs so, accordingly, I was put to work at this. So, besides being a draftsman, I was a sign painter, too. During our work we always had our gas masks and helmets handy, for who knew when the Boche would give us a taste of gas or pepper our depot with bombs.

His next letter was more descriptive about the new workshop:

> …which is gradually developing into a studio, for on the walls I have some paintings I did. They are very much admired by the officers and men, if it doesn't seem boastful to say this. It is here that I ponder over my daily toil, whatever it may be, and dream too of the things I have seen, and make mental pictures which I hope some day to realize on canvas. You know when I get home I can carry on with my painting, and still become a great architect. Ha!

In his makeshift studio Dechant focused less on his frustrations with the Army and concentrated his spare moments on art instead. By painting, he was able to make the best out of a difficult circumstance. He wrote,

> I simply love to paint and draw, in my 'off duty' time. One finds so much here to see and think about, that the evenings I don't write, I lie in my bunk and dream away in pictures. Or some evenings when I feel real smart, I take to my feet and have a nice quiet walk.

M.B.DECHANT. '18

Environs de Chambéry, France. 1918

M.B.DeChant

"Having spoken to you in one of my previous letters about taking 'a leave,' I have finally experienced my dreams, and find myself surrounded this evening by great mountains, the 'French Alps.' The place I am in is Chambery..."

*Environs de Chambery*, Watercolor, 1918

On these walks, Dechant saw the beauty in nature and the native architecture. He wrote,

> There are so many things here that deserve attentions from an artistic point of view. These old villages present themselves before my eyes as if they were wonder books in which hidden treasures lie. The majority of the boys walk through them and don't look higher than the mud. Why, in these old tumbled down buildings with moss on the roofs and stones covered with ivy there is the essence of poetry, and I am sorry that I am not gifted along that line, for I feel the beauty in all my heart.

The only thing in the whole of France he found ugly, was the war itself.

> Yesterday was a very rainy day, but in the evening, just about 7:30, there was the most beautiful rainbow I ever saw. It stretched from one side of the heavens to the other in a perfect arc, and the colors were distinct throughout. It was then that I thought of the glory of nature, and to think that war and the destruction that goes with it ruins and devastates the works of God. Those beautiful fields and forests of France, which lie now in the battle area, and which at one time boasted of fairness and beauty no longer nourish the trees which gave shade to the weary one. There is instead desolation and destruction, horrifying the observer and not gratifying the desire for the beautiful.

Throughout the war, Dechant focused on art and beauty. Long after giving up hope of military advancement, he was promoted to the rank of sergeant. In his letter home afterward, he doesn't even mention the promotion, only the appellation changed. Just three weeks after his promotion, November 9, 1918, the Kaiser fled to exile in Holland. Two days later the most powerful radio in the world, atop the Eiffel Tower, flashed the news to the world: "Hostilities will cease on all fronts…"

Elated, Sgt. Dechant wrote home: "The was is Over! What do you think of that? Better than all that, I am coming home when they send me. I suppose you folks at home know more about the news than we boys, so all I would tell you would be useless. The Kaiser est fini, and all the French soldiers are going crazy."

Miles sent this pair of Christmas cards home after the Armistice.

*Christmas Cards,*
Ink, Pencil, Watercolor, 1918

More contemplative, but still joyous, he wrote home a few days later with words that summarize some of his experiences:

> Well, just think, this terrible war has actually come to a close. President Wilson and all of the American people and Allies have come to a realization of the great dream of a successful overthrow of the Kaiser and a permanent Peace. It is truly a time to rejoice and thank God for his great goodness. It is a marvelous proof that right must conquer in the end… It makes me feel fine to think that the boys over here have been victorious. They have added to the reputation of their forefathers who fought and served in previous wars. They have nailed with an extra nail into the hearts of the nations of the earth that 'This government for the people and by the people shall not perish from earth.' It is true that peace must be signed, and that is the only great final and ultimate end. But

the war is over, and it deserves a great deal of thanksgiving to our Heavenly Father who I know guided the Allies to victory. But in the merry-making of those who are living, we must not forget or turn our attentions away from the heroic dead who so bravely fought here. It is for them that we owe our prayers and other outward material signs of recognition of gallantry and bravery. They, those boys, actually saved the world. In times like this, I had often felt sorry that I was not more of a fighting man to take a decided part in the battles. But God saw otherwise, I believe.

And so it was that the war was over, and Dechant found himself waiting to go home, and waiting, and waiting. He had been ready to leave for Pennsylvania the instant the Kaiser fled, but the Army had other plans. They kept him waiting at Is-sur-Tille doing the same ordnance work he had been doing all along. While he impatiently passed the time, a bigger killer than the war itself was raging across five continents. The Spanish flu, which had spawned itself in the tight confines of trenches and troopships, was wreaking death among those usually most competent to resist disease. In the very young and the elderly, it was a typical flu; but in healthy 20-year-olds, it was a lung hemorrhaging virus, more lethal than any influenza previously known. He knew he was in grave danger of contracting it, and he did, as did his mother and many, many friends. He took care, as best he could, and recovered rapidly. His mother also recovered, but he lost many friends. By the epidemic's end more than 21 million worldwide had died from the flu, twice the number who had been killed during the Great War.

The flu was but the first in a series of strange twists that would end Dechant's French sojourn. He was still in limbo at Is-sur-Tille, the Army unwilling to release him. With almost nothing to do, his Army classification had risen to indispensable. Now with plenty of reading time, he happened across an article in *Stars and Stripes* magazine advising that men could apply for a furlough to study at one of the famous European universities. He read the words of Major George Gray:

Our Army of citizen-soldiers found itself at the end of the campaign in a foreign land which is a veritable treasure house of art of every description, one whose history is intricately laced with the history of art, a land which for ages has been producing masters and master works, a land replete with museums, schools and instructors of great gifts.

The stated objectives of the Fine Art Department connected with the American Expeditionary Forces University were to stimulate interest in art, to recognize native talent, and to encourage as well as to provide opportunity for higher grades of study for those with talent. Dechant and the Army were on the same wavelength for once. If he was to be stranded in France for another six months anyway, he might as well take advantage of any educational opportunities. He was instantly taken with the possibility of studying at the Ecole des Beaux-Arts, which was considered the preeminent school of art and architecture in the world. "Oh, how I would love to do this," he writes.

While his new plan percolated, he wrangled a pass to see Paris and visit the Ecole des Beaux-Arts. Vividly, he describes the characters in his train compartment on the way to Paris:

> Seated right opposite me was a very fine young looking lady dressed in black and wearing a veil. She had lost her husband in the war; seated next to her was a very homely-looking elderly woman who talked in a snappy sort of way, but in all she appeared very jolly. Her husband was seated next to her. In the corner of the opposite seat, and next to the window, was seated one of those fine old French peasant men. On his lap he had a wicker satchel in which he was carrying a nice fat goose home for the festive season. The satchel was fixed so that Mr. Goose could poke his head out and look around any time he chose, and I must say that it was a very curious sight to see the old gentleman talk to the goose, which at once would set everybody laughing. One time the old man fell asleep and Mr. Goose gave him a jab in the nose which, I am

here to say, woke up the old man who, not feeling at all pleased with the actions of the goose, started to scold the creature. But the only reply was a loud squawk from the fowl. This was such an interesting picture that I took out my sketchbook and made a sketch of the old man and the goose. Then I suddenly became engaged in making pencil sketches of everybody in the car and, I still believe, in the whole train, for there were faces peering over the back of my seat which I had not seen before. Everybody became interested and, I believe everybody in the coach had their face drawn. But they all made me sign my name together with 'An American soldier' at the bottom of each sketch. The time and ride from Tours to Paris did not hang heavy on my hands under such circumstances, for I found a great deal of pleasure in drawing and laughing along with the rest.

Looking up from his drawing pad, "I saw the last glimmer of twilight fade, and the cars, rolling from side to side, traveled through dense dark woods, and over moors and marshes to where lay, in its perfect beauty and wonder, this marvelous city." The sights of Paris impressed him greatly: the Cathedrale de Notre Dame, the Arc de Triomphe, Place de la Concorde, Tuilleries Gardens, the Champs-Elysees and, of course, the Louvre. He wrote of all these sights with reverential excitement. He saved his visit to the Ecole des Beaux-Arts for his last day in Paris. This was special. The school was located in a fine part of Paris on the corner of Rue Bonaparte and the Quai Malaquais just across the river from the Louvre. As he arrived sandbags were being removed in the courtyard, and he watched in amazement at the materialization of a Roman triumphal arch. All the buildings around him had facades based on classic examples of architecture. He took it all in, including the somber mood:

It is extremely sad around the Beaux-Arts school for the reason that 75% of the students lost their lives in the war. In the great hallway of the administrative building there are rolls of honour, and it is astounding to see so many names. France deserves a great deal of credit. Here were men at this school learning and preparing for greater things and then, when the bud was about to burst into fragrance in a lovely flower, it was cut down.

Though sobered and saddened by the melancholic mood of the Ecole des Beaux-Arts, he returned to Is-sur-Tille with a resolve. He wanted to study there, in a desperate way. To this end the Army was both his impediment and his means. When applications for the program became available, he filled out two. Neither the government nor the Army had ever embarked upon an arts educational scheme of this sort, and the foreseeable delays were vexing and intolerable. As he waited to hear about his applications and didn't, he became increasingly agitated. He writes, "I am certainly sick of the Army, which is entirely void of a refinement and beautiful life which I crave." As his frustration mounted, he considered abandoning his educational plan and asked his father to send affidavits from home, stating that his work there was indispensable and that he must return to the United States immediately. "I have not heard any more about the university work, and I suppose that is another of the Army's games – not to give it to anyone. Since receiving the affidavits, I want to come home more than ever." Out of frustration, Miles decided to abandon his plans to attend, what was now officially called, the Art Training Center at Paris. He put his affidavits before the commanding officer. Instantly he regretted this fast decision, made under duress. A week later he would write:

> I have given up a wonderful opportunity to study in Paris to get home earlier. If they don't release me here, I shall lose all and shall regret this wonderful opportunity all my life. I just am full of architecture and art, and every spare moment I have finds me drawing. I have probably made one of the greatest mistakes in my life by giving up a course such as this. It is done now, and I shall take it like a man.

This time, however, destiny came into play. After his unalterable change of course, he received an order from General Headquarters

AEF to go study architecture at the Art Training Center in Paris. He couldn't believe it. "Can you imagine studying architecture in Paris for 3 months! I have to pinch myself every now and then to see if it is really true. Ha!"

What had happened was this: in his initial excitement to attend school in Paris, he had filled out not one but two applications. The applications had been routed in different directions, one going through General Headquarters. It was from there that he received direct orders to go to Paris. Of the three AEF Art Training Schools, he had been selected to attend Pavillion Bellevue in Sevres between Paris and Versailles. This school had been reserved for the most highly qualified instructors and 200 students, the most it could accommodate; there were more than 10,000 applicants. Bellevue was organized into ateliers according to specialty: Ernest Piexotto headed painting, Solon Borglum chaired sculpture, and Lloyd Warren was overseer of the architecture atelier and acted as dean of the school.

"I love the beautiful and am happy when I can study it."

*Caen*, Watercolor, 1919

44

A jublilant Dechant made his way there with "a full pack, two musettes full of oil paints, watercolors and drawing instruments, toilet articles, and in my hand a nice juicy apple pie which cook made for me, and a portfolio containing the last of my sketches. Together with this I had two barracks bags full of clean and dirty clothes and books and everything, mostly what a genius will collect and a soldier won't need." Arriving at Bellevue, he was taken with the beauty of this one-time fashionable resort on a hill. Overlooking the Seine River, it was everything he hoped for.

> Why, doggone it, I don't believe it's true! It seems like a dream. We can go to Paris anytime, and I understand there will be sketching parties and beaucoup lectures at great centers such as Versailles and Fontainbleau. There is a company of service men here to do the work, such as cooking and keeping the place in shape, while we fellows study architecture and become absorbed in the beauties of France. I am telling you, it is the greatest opportunity here, and this is but the first evening here. I can readily see it is one of the marvelous and great undertakings of our dear country to give these boys this opportunity. They deserve it. N'est-ce pas?

Classes started on March 17, 1919. Dechant's teachers at Bellevue were all from his intended place of study, the Ecole des Beaux-Arts. His new professors gave him the same architectural design projects that the highest students there would undertake. His day started with a physical drill, then French class. At 11:20 a.m. the students had a guest lecture, someone different every day. One day it was from the professor of textile design at Glasgow University, showing beautiful old hangings and laces from the Orient. The next day a professor of architecture at Yale lectured on Byzantine and Romanesque architecture in France. After these lectures, the rest of the day would be spent in design. As each day came to a close, they would cap off with an 8:30 p.m. lecture, which would last until taps sounded at 10:30. Dechant was in his element, writing, "This is a glorious opportunity and, oh, if I could only have 48 hours in a day. I can't begin to do or see all I would like to!"

Every week brought a study trip to Paris, either to see exhibits or sketch. On one trip to St. Cloud, as he drew a crumbling piece of architecture, a black motor car with flapping Japanese flags whisked by him. He wrote:

Today [May 7, 1919] the Allies handed over the papers for Germany to submit to, and, as a matter of coincidence, as I sat sketching, motor cars and limousines loaded with the world's greatest men rode by on their way to Versailles…away up the long avenue we recognized President Wilson. We snapped those heels together and stood at military attention and, just as he passed, we saluted, and then President Wilson gave us the finest smile and fairly thrust his head out of his car and saluted us in return. I tell you, that was a sweet smile, one I shall never forget.

"We hiked back to a little country village by the name of St.-Wandrille, where exists an ancient abbey now in ruins but, Mother, the most fascinating and charming place I have ever been. These old Gothic remains, worn and crumbling, overgrown with moss, and bursting forth with glorious masses of flowers clinging to the old stones, seem to speak of poetry and tell of the days when within these old walls monks were there and saints were made."

*The Abbey at St.-Wandrille,*
Watercolor, 1919

The three months of study at Bellevue came to a close in the middle of June, and finally he was on his way back to Pennsylvania:

> Ha! Ha! I am the happiest fellow in the world because I am <u>coming home.</u> The boys who have been at Bellevue deserve to come home, for we all worked hard there. Mr. Warren, who was our dean, gave us a farewell with tears in his eyes. He hated to see the school at Bellevue, which had such a short but brilliant career, broken up so soon. I have certainly profited by my experience in the Army and at the few short months in school at Bellevue. I owe a profound debt to the Government of the United States and to all who have been my teachers and superiors. Well, good-bye, but not for long. I hope I will have a pleasant and successful voyage.

And so it was that he left France from the sunny port of Brest, on the last day of June, 1919.

"You know how Mont St. Michel looks. Well, this place took the breath out of me."

*Mont St. Michel*, Watercolor, June 1919

Engaged to be married. Circa 1920

# III

# Family Man

$M$iles was eager to resume the life he left two long years ago. First and foremost, he was impatient to be reunited with his family. A small contingent waited to greet his train at Reading's Outer Station. As he stepped onto the platform, Miles was astonished to see his arthritic mother spring out of her wheelchair and run to meet him. Tears of joy streamed down their faces as they embraced. The family was momentarily amazed: Mama had done the almost impossible, and she herself was unaware of her feat, her joy so complete at that moment. Then everyone else mobbed the returning soldier: father, sisters, brother, and future fiancée Sarah Garvin. Amidst all the excitement, Miles was now facing as many expectations as there were people standing on the train platform. Sarah, in particular, was waiting to ascertain details of their mutual future, whether their plans for a life together would be fulfilled. His father and his brother needed to know his career plans. Miles had stepped into a whirlwind.

Art, which had figured so prominently and was such an important part of his life in France both aesthetically and creatively, was being relegated to an uncertain future. He had written, "an architect should be an artist," but when would he find the time? At almost age 30 he felt the clock running, and within the year he and Sarah were formally engaged. His professional life was equally busy; his ambition, "to become a successful architect," began to take shape as he formed an independent architectural practice within the family firm. He had served enough of an apprenticeship in Philadelphia to realize how to run his own practice, but there were some false steps in his first year.

Miles' most important sales presentation of 1920 was a meeting with Thun and Janssen, two very prominent industrialists who had settled in Reading upon arrival from Germany and established their first firm in 1892. By the time 1920 had arrived, their knitting mill business was flourishing, and the partners were looking toward expansion. For Dechant this introductory meeting could be the beginning of a long relationship and a sinecure for his architectural work.

The meeting did not go well. Either Thun or Janssen asked a question along these lines: "Tell us Miles, you were over there, what'd you think of the way the war went?" Miles plunged in, "Well, we ended it too quick. When we had the Boche on the run, we should have gone all the way to Berlin." Miles saw the expressions on Thun's and Janssen's faces and was instantly mortified at what he just said. But as much as he tried to recover and recapitulate, the deal was scotched and the fledgling architect was shown the door.

In this learning environment, Dechant was married. Miles and Sarah pledged their vows on February 10, 1921 in her hometown, Lancaster, Pennsylvania. The wedding party filled Memorial Presbyterian Church located across the street from the family's row house. Her father was a church deacon, and after years of waiting, Sarah's parents gave their eldest daughter a beautiful and memorable wedding ceremony.

Starting their life together, the newlyweds moved into one of Reading's smallest apartments. Their first child was soon on the way, and married life in the confines of a studio apartment was a life style adjustment. To complicate the situation Miles embarked on a big project in the middle of the only room. He spread out his easel, paints and sketches and began to paint *Entrance to the Cloisters at St-Maclou*. The painting was

Miles made this preparatory sketch in Rouen, France with his back resting on the walls of a 16th Century charnel house (a mediaeval cemetery used during the Black Plague). Although not visible, the door frames of the half-timbered building have carved figures portraying *The Dance of Death* and other macabre motifs.

The painting refined his sketch by clarifying the composition; he pulled the projecting lamp, the dominant foreground element, away from the dominant background element, the central roof peak. He also added narrative details, a foreground scroll, and a smoking chimney. Studying the alterations gives some insight into Dechant's working methods and aesthetic.

*Entrance to the Cloisters of St-Maclou*, Oil, 1921

to be a belated wedding gift for his sister, Mary, who had married in his wartime absence.

The painting is one of Dechant's few stabs at a narrative work. Oddly he chose to paint a charnel house for his wedding present. The narrative story within the painting is a mystery. Perhaps he had intended a comment about the difficulties of trying to reconcile faith and the horrors of modern war. However, for Dechant, it became more a comment about the difficulties of narrative painting. He almost finished the painting, but stopped at the unfurled scroll. This was never painted; his pencil layout lines are still clearly visible on the raw linen. Why, with only this small piece left to paint, would he stop work? Any number of things could be conjectured; perhaps he became uncomfortable with what he was trying to say; or thought it inappropriate for a wedding gift. Whatever the reason, it sealed the door for him on any future narrative work. His experience painting the *Cloisters* must have been discouraging; not only was the painting unfinished, but it seemed to finish him. His will to make art was apparently damaged and would not resurface for almost six years.

The unfinished painting of the *Cloisters* was intended to be a belated wedding present for Miles' sister, Mary, who was married when he was in France. She waited more than 10 years to press Miles to deliver her wedding gift ⌐ at which point he simply pulled this older canvas off the wall and handed it to her.

*Bertolet's Saw Mill*, Oil, 1919

The smell of oil paint convinced Sarah they had to move. She was interested in finding a modern, practical house, and finding it quickly — and Miles wasn't. He wanted a historic property "with the things that really appeal to my heart and soul." As Miles admired one dirty, dilapidated place after another, their first child was born. They named their son William Garvin, in honor of both their families.

As the new mother cared for her baby, she became increasingly anxious to move. The house hunt dragged on until Sarah was willing to acquiesce to almost anything, and she did. The neighborhood kids called it the "old, haunted house." It was a boarded up structure that once was home to a long forgotten winery; the oldest house in Mt. Penn, dating to 1820. For Miles the architect, age was the attraction. The winery, and even its land, were challenges. Indeed the grapevines had given up on the thin rocky soil and had long since withered away. Inside the house, there was no kitchen, no bathroom; in fact there was no indoor plumbing whatsoever. The house only had four rooms, two upstairs and two downstairs. After signing a $4,500 note with a local lender, Miles had his work cut out. Sarah and the baby would not move in until the house had plumbing. Miles made good on this promise by building a new kitchen and bathroom in one tiny addition.

This carving represents two years of his spare time spent with a very limited set of chisels.

*Sideboard Panel,* Walnut, Mid-1920s

Dechant started painting — the house. Between the remodel, the baby, and establishing his architectural practice, the new father should not have even thought about taking on any more projects, but he started carving an elaborate piece of furniture for his wife. A glacially slow project, he carved the central back panel out of solid walnut in just under two years.

Miles and Sarah's second son was born on November 23, 1923, and they named him Donald Hagman, honoring his grandmother's family. These were happy years for the couple. Content with his life, Dechant may never have returned to art, had fate not interceded.

Holding his two boys, Bill (left) and Don (right), Miles was a devoted father. Back of house shown during construction work.

The spring of 1926 was memorable for its wisteria. Perfumed clumps of the purple flower hung like clusters of ripe grapes ⁓ in the attic. Miles had planted the flowering vine innocently enough, but the wisteria had a mind of its own, twisting over the arbor and on through the shingles, into the house. Miles loved it, but Sarah said she couldn't abide it as a houseplant. To eradicate the wisteria, the ceiling had to be opened and a second remodel naturally followed. Miles and Sarah decided to add a new wing to the house. The project commenced with the usual mess; plaster dust and chaos were everywhere. Sarah tried to cope with the dust as best she could in spite of a flu-like condition that resisted treatment. In a letter to her sister, Jean Garvin Miller, she closed "I have a lot of pain around my eye and in my cheek bone ⁓ in fact, most of us 'ain't what we used to be.'"

Philadelphia was hosting the Sesquicentennial Exposition that summer, but Sarah did not feel well enough to attend. So Miles went alone and became entranced with the exhibitions. He returned twice more on successive weekends to soak in the excitement and admire the art and architecture of the different pavilions. This would be the first time he saw a new style of architecture called French moderne, today known as art deco. It appealed greatly to him. He had read about the French moderne style and its introduction the year before, in Paris, at the Exposition des Arts Décoratifs et Industriels Modernes. He brought home souvenirs for Sarah and regaled her with stories of the fair.

The marriage of Miles' sister, Sarah, to Harold Hauck was the other diversion from his wife's health problems during the summer of 1926. She was conspicuously absent from this wedding photo where every other sibling and spouse were present.

*Top row (left to right):* Miles Dechant, Arthur Schultz, Fred Dechant. *Center Row:* unidentified best man, Elizabeth Hartman Dechant, Harold Hauck, Sarah Dechant Hauck, Mary Dechant Schultz. *Bottom Row:* flower girls Judy Dechant, Dorothy Dechant.

Her interests were lagging, and she kept returning to her physician with complaints. She was pregnant again, and Dr. Muhlenburg treated her for everything seemingly under the sun. However, he was never able to diagnose her real problem. She continued losing weight into Indian summer and, in frustration, Miles insisted that she change doctors.

Miles had not painted a thing since 1921, but for his sister, Sarah, he decided to go all out. He and his younger sister, the singing diva, always had been particularly close with their similar sunny personalities. Wanting to give Sarah a painting of France, he dusted off some of his old sketches for inspiration. Although Miles painted this gift, it did not signify a return to art making ~ it was a blip in his artistic hibernation.

*French Chateau*, Oil, 1926

With a new doctor came a new diagnosis ~ cancer. In a time when cancer was almost untreatable, Miles went into a state of denial, desperately believing she could recover. But Sarah sensed otherwise, and she did not want her children to see her so ill. She felt that she should return to Lancaster and her parents' home as this could be a long stretch. Reluctantly, Miles shut down their home in Mt. Penn, packing things up as best he could. The young boys, then three and five, remember leaving the house with their mother for the last time, a pile of toys still left in the middle of the living room. The family of four took a sad drive to Lancaster.

The plan was for Sarah to see a new doctor in Lancaster and conva-
lesce. Miles and the boys were to return to Reading and stay with his
parents, who would care for the children while Miles continued working and commuting to Lancaster on evenings. On the weekends, Miles
took the boys to see their mother.

Forced to wait for these visits, Sarah spent long days resting in her old
childhood room on the second floor of their row house. When the boys
came running up to see her, she was happiest. Miles would stay by her
side, long after every one else was in bed, and he would say hopeful
things like, "Now you're feeling better, aren't you dear?" She was not
getting better, and she tried to tell him, but Miles was never ready to
believe his wife could be taken from him. So he sat next to her bed in
a rocking chair and just rocked — back and forth, back and forth.
Eventually all his rocking became irritating, and Sarah had her sister
remove the rocking chair. Miles was reduced to sitting there in a plain
wooden chair, doing that thing he did best — worry.

He was right to worry. Her doctor in Lancaster, Dr. Atley, believed that
her baby had died in the womb, causing a cancerous growth, which
might be removed in an operation. The surgery was scheduled for Nov.
23, her second son's birthday. Her baby had indeed died, and the doctor took it from her; he continued with exploratory surgery, only to find
her liver consumed with cancer. At that point, he closed the operation
without any further course of action.

Going into the operation, there still seemed to be hope. After the operation, the doctor offered none: what had probably begun as a breast
cancer had spread to her internal organs. After the shock of reality,
Sarah accepted the doctor's findings. In extreme pain, she asked to stay
in the hospital.

The two small boys William and Donald — then called Sonny and
Buddy — visited her there the first week of December. She had sent
someone out to buy toys, two red cast iron dump trucks, which they still

remember. The lifetime of love she wanted to give them was symbolized in these toys. Sarah, Miles, and the children all cried. Later, when she watched Miles lead her boys out the door, the younger son turned and said, "I love you, Mommy." That was the last time she saw her family. At the very end of 1926, just 17 days before Christmas, Sarah passed from this world and the lives of her family.

She left her children and husband to carry on life without her, and they didn't know how. Miles was, in the words of Sarah's sister Jean, "A grand mess, for a long time." He was seriously depressed and in the first weeks, the family was worried that he would not come out of it. Much less hardship had driven him to nervous breakdowns earlier in his life, and he was surely at these crossroads again. No doubt sensing this, his father walked into his son's old bedroom and told Miles he must get hold of himself. He literally ordered him out of bed.

He gave another order: build a Christmas present for your sons (who still were being cared for by the Garvin family in Lancaster). A great believer in the restorative power of God and railroads, he suggested Miles make a train table. Miles forced himself to walk into the garage workshop and set to work. While fighting through his grief, he put together an elaborate electric train table that was joined by ribs, dowels, screws, and x braces, bolted through with disparate and non-identical parts indexed alphabetically. On Christmas eve, he drove to Lancaster with the train table strapped to the roof of his Oakland sedan. While his boys slept, he set-up the magnificent gift that had been occupying his time and grief. Running on top of the table was an Ives Electric Switcher, a first class O gauge railroad. The toy train table was placed in the Garvins' parlor for the Christmas morning surprise and later moved with the boys to their Dechant grandparents' home. There, under the living-room window, the children could look up from their toy, directly out to the real trains steaming in from the Outer Station. The trains distracted and delighted the children. His father, William, had been right in suggesting the gift. It seemed to restore, in both his son and grandsons, the glimmer of hope.

Forced to focus on his children, Miles had less time to dwell in his own grief. He, like others who have suffered a profound loss, found inward reserves of strength that kept him going. After Christmas, he returned to work. Deliberately, his father kept supplying Miles with more and more projects, completing the design work on several residences and a new Dechant office building.

The next step toward emotional recovery was to reorganize his family life. He began looking for a housekeeper who could help him raise his children. He made sure to have his boys present when he interviewed different nannies. In March or April, Dechant found an older German woman named Ida, and the boys took to her right away. Miles moved out of his parents' house and, with Ida's help, reopened his Mt. Penn home. She was a good fit – Ida knew how to take care of children (having raised two sons of her own). She had an instant rapport with the young boys. She was industrious, the kind of woman who believed in spring and fall cleanings every year – everything would be moved outside and beaten with a broom. She took instructions literally: if their father said "It's a cold day, make sure the boys wear coats," she would have them wear those coats all day long no matter how hot it became. Still, she was a compassionate woman who saw these two boys without a mother and filled the gap to the best of her ability.

As his life became reorganized, Dechant's newly found free time once again played host to grief and melancholia. Miles was relapsing and desperately needed something to fill the void left by his wife. He decided to take the boys for a weekend at Mt. Gretna. While that was the highlight of their summer vacation, it didn't make him feel much better. Everything there, the yellow shingles, the hemp fiber carpets, the lake and summer theater, brought back vivid memories of Sarah. He needed something else. Art had helped to heal him during his college breakdown. Art had bolstered his spirits in France. By the end of 1927, after a six-year hiatus, he was ready to return to art again.

This little etching was adapted from a sketch of Nevers, France, where he was first stationed. "The more I look at this country what little I can see, and the surroundings, the more it fascinates me. I love artistic things, and here we find them in rarest quality." November 17, 1917

*15th Century Stair Case Tower; Nevers, France, Etching, 1927*

# IV

# A New Beginning

Taking an entirely different artistic direction, Dechant purchased an etching press. Etching presses were, and still are, expensive and heavy; so buying one implied serious commitment to a new art medium. He ensconced the behemoth in his bedroom, the only place in the house where there was enough room. The ventilation there was dismal, but he never seemed to mind the noxious fumes he created. While his children fled from the smell of nitric acid biting into the copper plates, he happily sloshed chemicals. Once again, he was in his element, never seeming to mind that the whole set-up was far from ideal. He began to make art. *(Page 63)*

The etchings he made that year were an austere contrast to his light filled paintings of France. Now he was producing small works of art, measuring 4 or 6 inches wide; he reduced color filled landscapes into meticulously hatched ink lines. Something about this monochromatic medium was well suited to his melancholic mood. He etched his Christmas card in 1927. It was a 15th century stair case tower in Nevers, France, and he was clearly thinking back to happier days.

The etching press was a distraction, and provided him an emotional outlet, but it was not a complete panacea. Despite his housekeeper's positive presence, Dechant continued drifting into deep worry about his children. For their sake, he became more committed to church and began every Sunday at St. Paul's Memorial Reformed Church. First there was Sunday school at 9:45 a.m. and then the 11:00 service. Miles and his children sat with his father, who held a listening aid to his ear, in a pew that held only four. The family's matriarch was too crippled by arthritis to attend, and other family members sat in pews behind them.

Miles' original design.

Upon its completion, Miles etched this commemorative program cover and then casually doodled on it.

After church the extended family gathered at the grandparents' home at 535 North Fifth Street where they were served an elaborate mid-day dinner, prepared by the live-in maid. As many as 15 family members could be around the table each Sunday. As quickly as the cousins could finish the roast beef, they would be excused and off to play. This would leave the adults alone to devour a political platter of after-dinner arguments. Miles did his best to avoid these confrontations by remaining affable and middle-of-the-road. The exceptions to his neutrality were his strong opinions about art and architecture.

In 1928, he was the architect hired to oversee a new façade and interior remodel of St. Paul's Memorial Reformed Church. He was pleased to be redesigning the family church as it partially fulfilled his longtime ambition to someday build one. As church projects are prone to do, it went over budget, through no fault of Miles. The church's members, in their pre-Depression enthusiasm, purchased a Skinner organ for $40,000 and requested many changes to the original plans. The project slowed as the church scrambled for a loan to fund additional construction. After one Sunday dinner, the patriarch asked Miles, "Why do you need a fancy church like that, when you can conduct your services in a tent?"

Miles left the middle of the road. Taking violent exception, he said, "You need a building that is commensurate with the importance of the occasion. You must have a well designed building to worship in!" This rare debate between father and son continued off and on until the project's end. Miles commemorated its eventual completion with an etching for the church's program cover.

Dechant continued to find solace in his etchings and focused his art exclusively on this mechanical medium for the next few years. He was learning how to speed up the process. He started ganging together several etchings for the trip into nitric acid. Chemical fumes mixed with his ever present pipe smoke never bothered the artist. He usually left the windows closed in his bedroom-cum-workshop, an atmosphere only he could have tolerated.

Etchings from 1927

Looking for new subject matter to etch, he began taking trips to the Oley Valley farmland, just east of Mt. Penn. One day he saw a for-sale sign on the type of rustic farmhouse he loved. His curiosity was piqued, and he made inquiries. For $1,500 he could buy the small, square stone house beside the Manatawny Creek which was devoid of all comfort facilities such as water and electricity. When he enthusiastically told his family about his find, they were appalled he would even consider it. Practicality was not Miles' concern; he saw the artistic and architectural potential in the old stone house. He allowed the family to talk him out of it, however, and used his entire savings instead as a down payment for the empty lot adjoining his home. He envisioned developing the lot by designing and building homes there in future days. He signed the papers just weeks before the stock market crash of October 24, 1929.

Although Miles had no money invested in the stock market, the crash did hurt him directly as his wealthy clients immediately stopped building. His savings had been spent on the lot. As the prospect of finding new work became increasingly bleak, a huge government project appeared on the horizon. Berks County, whose seat was Reading, had decided against remodeling and expanding the existing courthouse. Instead the powers-that-be decided to build an entirely new courthouse that would be large enough to house the proceedings of the whole county. The commissioners had been debating the merits of different sites and designs for three years and finally began to ask for the first proposals at the end of 1929.

In the past, Dechant had secured the majority of his jobs on the basis of his reputation, but the courthouse project was different. A half dozen architects were competing intensely for the big project, including his chief rival, Fred Muhlenberg. Not only did Dechant dislike Muhlenberg's style, but this man was also the brother of the doctor who had failed to diagnose his wife's cancer in its early stages. Muhlenberg brought out his competitive side. Dechant called the courthouse, "a job of a lifetime." Not only would it fulfill his dream of designing a cathedral-like skyscraper, but also it would provide years of work for both his architectural practice and his family's engineering firm in a deteriorating economy.

Dechant went alone to submit his courthouse proposals, armed only with an architectural rendering. An impressive rendering was critically important, and Miles delivered a new one at every meeting. Once his final rendering had been handed in to the county, there was nothing for him to do but keep working and waiting to hear. As the months passed, he stopped etching and took an artistic pause.

*Berks County Courthouse,*
Pencil rendering, 1930

On "the basis of its beauty," Dechant was notified that his courthouse proposal had been selected. From that moment, at the very end of 1930, his professional life had validation. With it, Miles seemed to lose the baggage of grief he had been carrying around, and a lightness of spirit carried over into his art.

Over the rest of Christmas vacation, Dechant embodied the old adage "If you want something done, give it to a busy man." He started painting again and broke through the barrier that went up in 1921 when he abandoned the *Cloisters at St. Maclou.* It had taken almost 10 years to return to palette and easel, and it would take a while longer to gather momentum. But now at age 40 he was poised to make his mark, emotionally and artistically, as an architect and artist. He was himself again as he headed outside into winter snow to paint two significant paintings in an impressionist mode. He worked fast to capture the moment: that brief confluence of light and paint where abstract brushwork becomes an emotional photograph. These two paintings reflected his new insight, not adaptations of sketches he did in France, but full-fledged original works of American art. (*Overleaf*)

Plein air painting in winter was an exercise in survival as well as a challenge in capturing a scene before the weather shifted. It was an activity for the swift and hardy and a uniquely Pennsylvanian form of impressionism.

*Top*
*Winter on the Manatawny*, Oil, 1930

*Bottom*
*The Snow Squall*, Oil, 1930

Dechant scratched with newfound confidence directly onto the plate of his 1930 Christmas card without any preparatory sketches. As the printing process reverses the image, it is very easy to end up with unexpected consequences. Dechant accidentally reversed the letters H and I in the word Wishing. He would see the mistake on the first proof he pulled, but by then it was too late for a correction. He sent the cards out anyway, and no one (outside the family) seemed to notice the error.

*The Wondrous Star*, Etching, 1930

As the country plunged into the Great Depression, Dechant had five and a half months to complete the courthouse design and hand it over to the contractor. He assembled a team of 50 draftsmen and engineers. His project was done under the umbrella of Wm. H. Dechant & Sons. His father ran the business aspects, while his brother, Fred, became the chief civil engineer. Working with an army of talented people to execute his vision, the architect was in his element.

Two months into the construction of the courthouse, Miles hosted an outdoor Fourth of July party for all the family. After a dinner of hamburgers and watermelon, fireworks came out and one would have been hard pressed to differentiate the actions of the adults from their children – Miles excepted. He wanted to paint his father's portrait and placed his easel by two trees on the property line. With fireworks going

Originally an outdoor scene, Miles painted this portrait of his father during a rowdy Fourth of July party.

*Father*, Oil, 1931

off behind him, he concentrated on his seated father. He was serious about his work and oblivious to the growing rowdiness. His brother, Fred, who was holding an archer's bow, asked the children, "Have you ever seen anyone shoot an arrow out of sight?" Obviously not. He extracted an arrow from his quiver, pointed the bow straight up, and shot into the sky. The children gasped as it disappeared, and for a moment nothing happened – then it came back, fast! With a cutting sound, the returning arrow sliced through the ragtop of his new Packard. This caused a commotion to raise the dead, but unaware of all the turmoil, Miles painted away, long after the last firecracker had popped.

Later that night, Miles gazed at the painting, and he was not satisfied with his afternoon's work. "It's just not right," he told his boys. He pointed to the two tree trunks, painted on either side of his father. In the eyes of the artist, the portrait looked like an interior scene pasted onto an outdoor background. So he brought the canvas into his bedroom workshop and wiped away the trees, using a turpentine-soaked rag. In their stead he painted a quiet interior background. Now settled, he signed the painting. Without skipping a beat, he returned to his architectural work.

The Courthouse Project consumed his every waking moment for two more years. Architecturally, it was his greatest triumph. Towering 260 feet, it was the first and only skyscraper in Reading. Although art deco

The Berks County Courthouse stood in glorious isolation like a cathedral of old.

was not then used as a term, the building is now considered one of the finest examples of its kind in the United States. It was also the first art deco courthouse in the country. The towering spire and monumental carved eagles lent some resemblance to a modern cathedral. Supporting this analogy, the lobby was designed to simulate the nave of a Gothic church; the sandstone ceiling was carved into arching hollow vaults. It was the closest he would come to his life ambition of designing a cathedral. Each courtroom in the building paid homage to a different style of architecture: Federalist, Georgian revival, Greek, and Florentine. Dechant reinterpreted each of these classic styles in a modern vernacular.

The design was a success, and the community was proud of its new skyscraper. However, the Wm. H. Dechant & Sons firm did not utilize the profits accrued with the sound expertise that built the courthouse. The patriarch exercised poor judgment by investing the bulk of the proceeds in row houses flanking the railroad tracks, railroads being his lifelong preoccupation. The area was to turn into a slum within a few years. But Miles was unconcerned. He trusted his father, money was secondary, architecture was paramount, and the courthouse was a labor of love. Energized by its completion, his creativity burst forth in art.

Miles celebrated the courthouse's conclusion with the first and only self-portrait of his life. He set a shaving mirror in one of the pigeon holes of his mahogany desk, and etched himself in poor light. He wasn't satisfied with his first imprint; something about his right eye bothered him. He went back in several times and tried to correct the problem. Failing that, he signed the final attempt: Miles B. Dechant, Architect.

*Self-Portrait*, Etching, 1932

Every spare moment became his chance to paint; Saturdays he worked half the day, and he would race home anxious to get going. After a quick lunch, he would pack the boys into the car and seek inspiration in the Oley Valley. Only a 20-minute drive from Mt. Penn, Oley's farms were like stepping 100 or 200 years back in time. As the boys played and punched each other in the back seat, Miles would drive through the countryside dreaming. The youngsters could never wait to get out of the car and would badger him to stop. Patiently he'd tell them, "We'll stop when I find something picturesque." Picturesque is now an almost unused art term, but for Miles it was the goal. For a subject to achieve this status it would feature simple yet excellent architecture in a scenic and pastoral setting, but most of all it would be nostalgic. His eyes scanned the landscape looking for the magic ingredients, and when he found them, he would pull his 1930 Buick off the road in a cloud of dust and set out to capture his impressions in paint.

*Miles B. Dechant*

Entering the Oley Valley from Friedensburg Road, Bertolet's Saw Mill was one of the first scenic stops, and Miles often painted it.

*Saw Mill*, Watercolor, 1932

While the boys went to throw rocks or play in the stream, Miles set up either his old Julien easel for oil paint, or his new watercolor easel. If it were watercolors that day, he would bend down over the stream to fill up his old, green Army canteen. Then aligning himself directly in front of his subject, he would sketch rapidly and lay in his watercolors. After an hour or so of work, his first painting of the day would be complete. He would take a quick appraisal, but was rarely very content with his renderings. Then he would cut the finished painting off the top of the watercolor block (bundled papers with a gummed edge around them), and start again at a new angle. He was a restless painter who liked to move his easel around, always looking for a more perfect vantage point in his quest to capture the picturesque more profoundly.

Miles Dechant plein air painting. Taking watercolor paint outdoors posed some problems; the standard commercial easels are all wrong.  They are designed to hold the work upright, which is disastrous for water flow. Out of necessity, he developed a horizontal easel. He used the solid walnut leftovers of his abandoned sideboard project to create a functional art tool of original design and beauty. With just a few twists on the thumbscrews, it would unfurl itself from a tightly packed little box into a horizontal watercolor table on tripod legs. There was nothing he loved so much as setting it up in the Oley Valley.

Far too rapidly for Miles' liking, the day would be over. His combination of concentration and natural reverie made his minutes pass like seconds and his hours like minutes. Many times he found himself scrambling to capture his final impression of the day ⸺ a golden sunset. Painters call it the magic hour, that brief period of time when nature lets loose with all she has ⸺ orange and pink, purples and reds all gushing together for one brief moment. By the time last touches went on that final painting, Miles would be running late. He would quickly pack it in and head back to the world of deadlines, commitments, and family bickering.

The last painting of the day was often finished as the sun went down. He was fascinated by the play of changing light on water.

*Afterglow*, Watercolor, 1932

One Sunday in November of 1932, at the family dinner after church, the adult children were in an uproar over the presidential election. It seems only one member of their clan had voted for Franklin Delano Roosevelt, and it was their patriarch. William's children wanted no part of "the New Deal," and threw a fit in the direction of their father. Miles also was shocked by his father's vote, but stayed away from the arguments. Instead, he secluded himself on the sun porch to paint a portrait of his son. This in turn caused his sister, Mary, to become embroiled in a side argument with her father, the newly announced Democrat. She wanted to hook rugs on the day of rest, and he would not allow it. She demanded to know why Miles was allowed to paint, and she couldn't "paint with rags." William Dechant was having none of his children's mutiny and was becoming more and more agitated until he suddenly had "palpitation of the heart." His wife interceded, "Now, Papa lie down!" So William lay on the couch, very still. The whole scene suddenly calm and quiet, the family waited for their

William age 11 (in those days called by his middle name Garvin) on the sun porch.

*Portrait of Garvin*, Watercolor, 1932

father's heart to resume its normal rhythm. Then they resumed their contentions, as if it were nothing but a time-out.

Oblivious to all this hysteria was Miles. He returned later from the sun porch with his watercolor, and interrupted the ongoing argument to have his painting critiqued. More fun for the family, they offered up their typical criticisms while the artist listened stoically: "Miles, the color is all wrong," or "Why don't you move his head closer to the top edge?" Miles weathered these indignities with a sense of humor, puffing on his pipe and only replying indirectly, as if heeding the admonition to suffer fools gladly. He would say "Uh hum," or "My, my," until the family's interest in his painting wavered and the political harangue resumed.

Miles continued to harbor reservations about Franklin Delano Roosevelt, and they were confirmed on March 5, 1933. FDR closed the banks to halt failures across the United States. He came home that day and leaned heavily on the kitchen door. "We're wiped out," he announced, "we lost everything." Within weeks of his bank loss, he regained his composure, and came to terms with it. He had never been overly concerned about money, and he was determined not to start now. He chose to remain optimistic that things would work out for the best.

His art was becoming more experimental. When he ran etchings they were likely to be aquatints or sugarlifts or drypoints. He would go into the attic and make weird concoctions for the sake of staining a frame, or toning some paper. Dechant called his boys up to the attic one day to watch him "antique" his diploma. In amazement they watched as he dipped his fine, large architectural degree from the University of Pennsylvania into an unpleasant mixture of coffee grounds, burnt umber, and ammonia. He sloshed the diploma around a bit and then pulled it out, looking rather satisfied. It was never really the same after its "antiquing" (the boys thought it looked wrinkled and smaller). But the artist loved that look.

## Three from 1933

Right
*Log House with Red Porch*,
Watercolor

Opposite, top
*Pennsylvania Haystacks*,
Watercolor

Opposite, bottom
*Covered Bridge at Pleasantville*,
Oil

Miles B. Dechant

January through September 1933, was the most artistically productive period of Miles' life. In that short burst, he made about 60 paintings and 5 etchings. As art was becoming a more important part of his life, his friendships with other artists were more significant. He was a member of the Reading Sketch Club, "a loose as ashes organization," which met once a month on Wednesdays for figure studies and socialization. There were about 20 members but only about 10 ever showed up. A few years earlier, when the club needed to find a new meeting place, Dechant volunteered the vacant third floor in the Dechant Building.

He built a black draped model's stand, arranged lighting, and placed drawing benches around the room. For this magnanimous gesture, he was voted president of the Reading Sketch Club. None of Dechant's Sketch Club work seems very engaged, however. There could have been a time constraint problem or perhaps he was uncomfortable with nudity (he told his boys that he would paint clothes on the nude models). Since he rarely included figures in his paintings, there is good reason to believe the Sketch Club's main attraction was camaraderie.

*Spanish Dancer,* Watercolor, 1932          *The Fencer,* Conte Crayon, 1933

James Luft worked as the club's de facto proctor, who took time away from his own work to walk the room and give helpful tips and encouragement to others. Dechant had much in common with him. There were two Luft boys roughly the same ages as his own, and Mrs. Luft was pleasant and welcoming. Luft was also a musician, a puppeteer, and a sociable fellow. At least twice a month, on weekday evenings, Dechant would take his children to visit Luft at his home. Never bothering to call ahead, they would drive 20 minutes to the old town of Wernersville

*Studio of James B. Luft, Artist,*
Watercolor, 1932

and take their chances. If Luft were home, his wife would watch the boys while the two artists went to the studio barn, behind the beautiful limestone house, to either etch or paint.

Dechant's other important art club friendship was with Ed Clymer. Clymer was a bachelor living on Clymer Street in Reading. If the street name seems to imply he was successful or famous, that's exactly the affect Clymer was hoping to achieve. But such was not the case: he lived a bohemi-an life in an unkempt row house. He painted in his shirtsleeves and was quite a contrast to the proper Dechant who was seldom seen minus tie and coat. But appearances aside, Clymer was a skilled painter; Miles respected his work and valued his friendship.

In the summer of 1933, Miles agreed to drive Clymer to his vacation home in Gloucester, Massachusetts, and stay on for two weeks of paint-ing. Although he had briefly visited Gloucester in 1928, this was his first long vacation since the days of Mt. Gretna. He was in high spirits when they packed up his 1930 business coupe with all their equipment and sup-plies and headed off on the 400 mile trip. Clymer espoused his color the-ories on the drive up. Clymer believed in a vivid palette, and Dechant's paintings from this trip show his influence. Miles normally muted his col-ors, but on this trip he used pure undiluted strengths and had difficulty achieving the color harmonies that previously came so naturally. Many paintings from this trip suggest the artist lost the struggle.

While Clymer's advice might have been hyper-chromatic, he did understand the workings of the art world better than Dechant and encouraged him to start entering exhibitions. Following this advice, when Miles returned from vacation, he made frames for the best of his Gloucester and Oley Valley paintings. He also built a rough and splintery pine crate to contain them. He addressed the crate to the Pennsylvania Academy of the Fine Arts in bold, black calligraphy. From this first group of paintings, the jury selected one for inclusion in their 1933 Watercolor Exhibition. The chosen work was *Tied Up*, a high angle, tightly cropped watercolor impression of a schooner.

## Gloucester Group

*Top*
*Cape Ann*, Watercolor, 1933

*Right*
From his rowing days Dechant liked boats and was comfortable painting them.

*Repairs*, Watercolor, 1933

*Opposite*
His first juried painting at the Pennsylvania Academy of the Fine Arts.

*Tied Up*, Watercolor, 1933

More important to the artist, even than the acceptance of his painting into a respectable show and his friendships, were the hours Miles could spend alone — painting in the countryside. In nature, God gave Miles his greatest inspiration. He was fascinated and respectful of rural life. "The farmer's life," he wrote, "is after all, the only right life, and it is surely the most healthful." In paint, he managed to convey this reverence. *Wine Making in the Oley Valley* captures the mood of a languid summer day. The winery dominates the farmers, and in turn nature dominates the winery. The roiling clouds suggest the winds of change. The deep forest on the right side of the winery, painted in a brilliant impressionistic slather of quick marks and daubs, frames the subject in deep mystery.

In the beautiful farms of the Oley Valley, Miles found "the contrast and consequently the beauty between man's humble and insignificant works as compared to the mighty works of our creator."
*Wine Making in the Oley Valley*, Oil, 1933

Whatever farming ambitions Dechant had, they were best realized in his paintings. In his own garden he was as likely to meet disaster as he was growth. That summer's planting season had started with zinnias and high hopes. By late summer, the flowers attained good height and were blooming when Dechant realized that all the leaves were coming off at the lower levels. He held the tattered leaves in his hands and shook his head. "Very unusual," he said. He could not fathom what was happening to his zinnias, until he pulled in from work one afternoon and happened to see a pack of dogs in his back yard chewing on the leaves. Every neighborhood dog, from Dachshund to Dalmatian to mongrel, was relishing the zinnia smorgasbord. That ended the zinnias. Defeated by flower-eating dogs, Dechant went inside and lay on the couch.

By the end of summer 1933, he needed rest. More than just the zinnias, two years of unprecedented creativity had taken their toll and left him artistically drained. He was exhausted. As he teetered on the edge of another serious depression, his artistic production suddenly crashed. He stopped painting entirely and made two somber etchings of a broken canal lock.

*Schuylkill Canal at Gibraltar*, Etching, 1933

*Schuylkill Canal at Gibraltar*, Etching (2nd version), 1933

Dechant returned to paint the Schuylkill Canal the following year in a different mood, and achieved a drastically different affect. As much as his mood had changed, so also would his life.

*Schuylkill Canal at Gibraltar*, Watercolor, 1934

# V

## Sunday Painting in Troubled Times

The enchanted bubble of creativity that had surrounded the courthouse project had burst. His joyous and productive Saturday afternoons painting in the Oley Valley were seemingly over. Instead his avocation of choice on Saturday afternoons turned into napping on the living room couch. The effects of the Great Depression were catching up to him. For Miles, challenging jobs were practically non-existent and his bread-and-butter work was in designing modest homes that presented little architectural challenge. The fees he took were commensurately low, and after the courthouse project, he seldom accrued more than a modest income. No doubt, these financial worries negatively impacted his art life.

Even beyond personal finances, which Miles could usually ignore, this unwelcome return of depression seemed to have its roots in loneliness. Since the death of his wife he had struggled as a solo-parent, without any other adult companionship. In one of his few 1934 paintings, this loneliness manifests itself subtly in paint. He returned to paint the *Schuylkill Canal at Gibraltar* again. In this work, everything in the painting was lovingly paired, the two partners in the rowboat, the bridge and its reflection, and even the homes. (*Opposite*)

Envision two buildings in a painting: they share the same scene, but can seemingly never change location. For years Miles had been aware of an attractive young woman who attended church as faithfully as the Dechant family. Every Sunday he would notice Dorothy Kachline in the pew across the aisle. As he sat between his children and his father, listening to the sermon, Miles sometimes caught her eye. They would smile at each other, nod politely, and Miles would continue his habitual doodling on the church program. Usually father William, while not approving, tolerated his son's aimless sketching. But one Sunday the pastor, Dr. Creitz, was giving an especially vigorous sermon. He had the elder Dechant's blood pumping, and his son's infernal doodling became too much — it detracted his attention from the "complete commitment!" being called for from the pulpit. This adverse stimulation led to "palpitation of the heart" for the patriarch. With his pulse racing wildly, William Dechant lay down, right then and there on the pew, as the sermon raged on. Miles and his boys scrambled for other seating. After the sermon's emotional discourse was over, William's pulse returned to normal and he was able to stand with the rest of the congregation. This scene with father William, while not a weekly occurrence, happened repeatedly in the course of his later years. After the service Dorothy, the other Dechants in the congregation, and many friends would inquire about his health.

The annual Sunday School picnic of 1934 changed the polite nodding at church into a true friendship. Miles and Dorothy arrived separately that day but soon were paired as partners in a race where the gentleman laid newspapers on the ground ahead of the lady as she walked toward the finish line. They were not remembered for winning the race, but they did spend the rest of the day together. Dorothy told him that she would be directing a church play in the near future and asked, "Could I get you to help with the scenery?"

Miles accepted the assignment as happily as bees fly to purple flowers on summer days. He painted the scenery for the play in the barn of another artist friend, Clint Shilling. And so, in a barn, by way of a church, romance was reborn for the lonesome father and widower. Dorothy was eight years younger than Miles, and her youthful presence started vanquishing the weariness that had been entangling his artistic soul. He returned to painting, and with his depression lifting, the need for Saturday napping was gone. The new relationship kept Miles busy, but they also found time as a couple for painting trips. Best for him were their journeys together into the Oley Valley where he could paint in the warm sunlight and cool breeze. As Miles painted, Dorothy read or knit. They would enjoy each other's quiet company as Miles peered through his bifocals either to study the scene or smile at Dorothy.

Dorothy, who had been baptized in the Moravian faith, encouraged Miles to paint Moravian churches and other historical sites. The Ephrata Cloister was one of America's first communal societies. Built in the 18th century, celibacy doomed it to extinction.                    *The Cloisters at Ephrata*, Watercolor, 1936

Their relationship continued to bloom, and on June 22, 1935 they were married at St. Paul's. On the occasion, Dorothy remarked "I told the architect (during the renovation) that he should put in a center aisle, and today I walked him down it." The bridegroom's sons, Bill and Don, were the attendants of honor. Their honeymoon was spent on Staten Island, and Miles admonished himself to forget painting for once. But in the months following the wedding, he was able to paint frequently.

1935 Wedding Photo. From left: Bill, Miles, Dorothy, and Don.

By year's end, with the weather turning very cold, Dorothy stopped accompanying Miles on his weekly painting excursions. Undeterred, he ventured north one chilly day under less than ideal driving conditions. He had spent the better part of a cold afternoon painting, and feeling poorly he headed home. The light was fading as he drove through Cross Keys and saw a scene he could not resist. He turned around, and before leaving the security of the Dodge, he bundled up and packed his pipe with Prince Albert tobacco. After opening the car door, he attempted to generate some warmth by rapidly smoking his pipe and trying to ignore his hacking cough. Carrying easel and supplies across the snow, he left a fragrant tobacco trail as he searched for the perfect vantage point. Finding it, he set up his gear in the snow and set out to capture some impression of the blustery day. Always a fast painter, the cold drove him to lay in his colors at lightening speed. Forty minutes in, he was heading for the paper with yet another paint-laden brush when he suddenly stopped. He stopped because an instinct honed from 20 years of painting told him something. He saw on his watercolor paper a collision between blind accidental fate and consummate skill. It was the realization that everything went right; God almighty, the thing was perfect! Then came the dilemma all artists have faced since time began: would just one more dab of paint be better? But he knew from experience that, if so much as one dab is added, there will be a second, and third and so on until only the tantalizing memory remains of what once was. But still his brush hung in mid-air with his thoughts — which way to go? The smoke decided; he coughed for breath in the ice-cold air. When he stood up, the spell was broken. The painting was done, and he headed for the car. (*Overleaf*)

When Miles returned home and took a more thorough look at his painting, he knew it was good, maybe his best. But his joy was tempered by the realization that, however good the painting may be, his health was not. His cough, his wheezing, and his never-ending cold symptoms were wearing him down, and he vowed to quit smoking. He had tried to stop two years earlier, and two years before that; but this time, in the glow of his pipe, he vowed to fight his battle with tobacco to the end.

This would be his last smoke, so he threw his matches away. An hour clicked by. The second hour clicked slower still. The third hour moved like lead. He could think of nothing except smoking. He remembered a game he would play when his children were little: the case of the disappearing smoke. He would inhale, put the pipe to his ear, and blow smoke from his nose. At work he thought about pipes, and the following day he thought about cigars. He came home and thought about smoking while he paced up and down waiting for dinner. Sitting down to eat, he was visibly angry. Finally he erupted, "Nobody's noticed anything about me tonight." His family rewarded him with blank stares. Unhappy with the lack of recognition his tobacco abstinence was receiving, he announced: "It's been three days, I haven't smoked in three days!" Miles was nothing like himself; his sunny personality had turned upside down. Four days, five days later, and he still couldn't taste his food. Steak tasted like mushrooms and vice versa, and he was getting grumpier and grumpier. He thought about what his doctor had told him, "… that's not just a bad cough, Miles. That's a heart cough." He fought with his addiction and his conscience. He felt guilty about the

*Afternoon at Cross Keys*, Watercolor, 1935

This quick painting was Dechant's most widely exhibited work. In general he tended to exhibit watercolors and not oils, which leads to the question: was he primarily a watercolorist? His tendency to exhibit watercolors may say more about the system than the artist. Then, as now, there were more watercolor societies and watercolor shows overall. The smaller size of watercolor paintings made them easier to ship for judging in the days before slides were used. In contrast, the whole oil painting process was more cumbersome. But when he made an important painting as a wedding gift or commemorative remembrance, it was always in oil.

first time he smoked a corncob pipe, he felt weak, he felt desperate, and he felt sick. It had been a week of hell, and his good intentions were defeated. Miles struck a match and the battle was lost — yet again.

Others in the family were having health problems that year. His father, by family consensus, had "become confused." William, at age 85, was increasingly difficult when he came into work, demanding immediate updates on jobs that had been finished years earlier. Senility, if anything, made him especially unwilling to concede a point. Miles was shaken by his father's actions and found himself in a quandary, weighing his father's dignity against the need to stabilize the company. Miles' brother, Fred, felt equally conflicted, but together (as gently as possible) they removed William from any real involvement with the business. The brothers' first major business decision outside their father's sphere of influence was to cash out on the Dechant Building. The sale helped recoup some of the losses sustained from William's real estate investments. Miles decided to stick with his brother and they rented a smaller office on Franklin Street, still doing business as Wm. H. Dechant & Sons. Out of respect to their father, his roll-top desk was kept in a back room and Fred was particularly good about bringing his father in to "look" at papers. Mentally he continued to deteriorate, descending deeper into senility with each day.

In November 1936, William Dechant's offspring went to vote at the polls and left their father at home, lest their father get one last crack for Franklin Delano Roosevelt. When he was re-elected, anyway, the conservative Miles took it with characteristic political indifference and even a detached ironic amusement. After all, the socialists already ran his own hometown, from Mayor J. Henry Stump on down. Reading was one of only three socialist enclaves in the United States, so having a socialist for a president (as Dechant saw Roosevelt) was just the final nail in the waiting coffin. Miles' principle objection to socialist programs, created for the benefit of blue-collar workers and (the votes of) labor unions, was that they were inequitable to professional workers.

Although Miles disagreed with many of Roosevelt's policies and programs, he found himself in competition for them. The Works Progress Administration (WPA) was building a music pavilion for the City of Reading. He needed the work, anticipated its theatrical possibilities, and wanted a chance to "present a series of transitions from the rough work of nature to the smoothness and perfection of the skilled work of man." Since these projects were awarded on the basis of politics as much as architectural renderings, Miles the architect needed to make a peace offering to the socialists at city hall. He did this via the Registrar of Voters, who now recognized him as a Democrat. His re-registration tactic was successful, thus allowing his design to be considered for its own merits. The music pavilion, more commonly known as the band shell, was ultimately awarded to him.

Dechant's art was as conservative as his politics, but unlike politics where he could be indifferent or even change his voter's registration while remaining middle-of-the road, he had strong opinions about art and architecture. These he would not compromise. He revealed his conservatism visually through his entire body of work. But there is also a first-hand account, in his own writing, commenting on his aesthetic and artistic agenda. He had been queried by the French magazine *Revue Des Arts* after their critic saw Miles' painting *Afternoon at Cross Keys* at the Philadelphia Academy of the Fine Arts. The critic writing the article asked Dechant for information on his "life work, education, preference in the arts, press cuttings, photographs, etc." Dechant's handwritten response offers some brief, but fascinating confirmation of his artistic conservatism. Writing about himself in the third person, Dechant replied: "He despises the ultra-modernists, and feels it will not endure. His preference in the arts is of the restrained modern school in both architecture and painting."

Today, it strikes one odd that Dechant called his style "restrained modernism," when he was so clearly working in an impressionist mode; he was painting in plein air, using the impressionist grammar of free almost abstract brushwork, and tying to capture a certain quality of daylight, moment, and implied realism. But Miles was probably using the

Volunteer Fireman's Memorial Music Pavilion (Band Shell). Photo from the 1980's

vernacular of the day in describing his style of work. He was in the company of other Pennsylvania impressionists who worked in similar modes; they did not consider themselves impressionists either. Even Miles' former teacher, Daniel Garber, hated to be called an impressionist (according to Brian H. Peterson, Senior Curator at the James A. Michener Museum of Art). So too, Edward Redfield, the dean of Pennsylvania Impressionism, disliked being thought of as anything other than a completely wonderful and original painter. Most of these painters had so much ego and individuality that they refused to think of themselves as part of an "ism." And by the 1930s, impressionism was seriously out of vogue; artists were leery of using its label, lest they appear regressive.

Dechant was aware of "ultra modern" styles as he saw them alongside his own work at exhibitions. His painting *Afternoon at Cross Keys* traveled by invitation to the Art Institute of Chicago in the spring of 1937. There his painting hung with some of the foremost and well recognized modern painters: Picasso, Klee, Kandinsky and Grosz. Standing in front of the modernists' work he would sigh, "tut, tut, tut," and solemnly shake his head in disapproval. He did not want to be challenged or assaulted by someone else's viewpoint; he thought that job should be left to the politicians not artists. In other words, he did not view art as a political statement. He thought the chief aim of art should be beauty and harmony. He preferred artists who made picturesque, well crafted works of art that could transport the imagination to a place of beauty. And he thought ultimately, the permanent value of art lay in its ability to preserve a record of life as it was lived or had been lived in earlier times.

In that aspect, he was akin to a historian or preservationist. An excerpt from an article he wrote about the conservation of architecture explains his position on art equally well:

> We cannot remember our forefathers without remembering their architecture. It is just as important to preserve old buildings as it is to keep history. In tearing down fine old buildings that were built by our forefathers we commit a great crime. What rights have we to molest the stones they laid or the timbers they hewed all with honest and most sincere toil? Can our children remember them if everything they did is thrown to the four winds? The history of a country depends to a large extent upon the character of its architecture, for it is through that we can study the habits, customs, and lives of past peoples and generations. Are we to throw everything away? And exclaim, 'It isn't modern!' You will say that we cannot advance. But surely we cannot advance if we do not take care of the art treasures which are our heritage and have been given our safe keeping.

Having written this homage to preservation, Dechant was not without his contradictions. In late 1937, he decided to start collecting the hand-made ceramic-roofing tile that covered old barns. He liked the look of the old tile, and wanted to cover his planned home expansion with them. So on the weekly painting trips to the Oley Valley, Miles would spot barns covered with old tile and approach the farmers and offer to buy their 100 to 200 year-old roofs. Usually the farmers jumped at the chance to dump their old leaky barn tiles onto a city chump; they knew a good corrugated roof was better on a barn. Miles would send one of his sons scrambling to the top of the barn to pry off the tiles. As he watched the very old tile being tossed down and loaded into the pick-up truck borrowed from his father-in-law, he didn't seem worried about the barn's preservation. He loved holding the ancient tiles in his hands and letting them transport him back into time. Never mind that the project was a huge mess and a giant storage problem.

Dechant had designed many prestigious buildings in his life, and by 1938 had achieved a good measure of success as an architect, by anyone's standards. But recognition from the art world proved more elusive. His obscurity was not helped by his reluctance to sell paintings. He hated to "let one go." Typically he would only sell in moments of great need, and then mostly to family. He wanted it both ways: to keep his paintings at home and establish his reputation at the same time. It was the artistic equivalent of having your cake and eating it, too. Dechant could not understand why he could not have both. The situation frustrated him. Regardless of his purposeful lack of sales, he set out to establish his reputation in the fine arts as he had done in architecture. Consequently, he spent more time painting; he listed himself in the *2nd Volume of Who's Who in American Art*; he had a two-man show at Buck Hills Falls resort shared with the well known painter of seascapes, Frederick J. Waugh; and he set out to expand his connections in the art world by going farther afield.

The Oley Valley had so many minor roads going off in all directions that even Miles made new discoveries. In the late 1930s he found Basket, a cluster of houses and the name of a road. He went back many times to paint there. Before he set up to paint a house, Miles very often asked the owner for permission. Some people were suspicious, some couldn't be aroused, some showed up after the painting was begun. All were curious and often spent time watching Miles paint while they pestered him with questions. Miles paid them minimal attention as he concentrated on his work.

*Fall in Basket*, Oil, Late 1930's

*Opposite*
*Winter in Basket*, Oil, Late 1930's

# BASKET THROUGH THE SEASONS

Now that his son Bill had a driver's license, Dechant could sit in the passenger seat and easily increase the range of his painting expeditions. He was finding more picturesque subject material and meeting other artists. In regard to making the acquaintance of fellow artists for the first time, it was an era where introductory phone calls were not the custom. Miles would drive far out of his way to "knock on the door and take my chances." It was in this way he met some of the better-known personages of the Pennsylvania art scene that year. He took a long drive to Chadds Ford to meet N.C. Wyeth. He also started painting in new locales: Bucks County, New Hope, and Center Bridge, home to the contingent of Pennsylvania Impressionist painters. On one of these trips to Center Bridge he met the renowned Edward Redfield. While today Redfield is still recognized by the cognoscenti, in his prime he was considered one of the greatest living American artists. From the turn of the century and extending into the 1920s, he exhibited more paintings and won more medals than any of his now much better known contemporaries including John Sloan and John Singer Sargent. He was 21 years Dechant's senior and had been considered the leader of Pennsylvania Impressionism while Miles was still in college. By the 1930s, however, he was no longer the powerhouse known only a decade earlier, but he was still active and Dechant wanted to meet him.

Taking his chances and knocking on the door, Dechant was delighted to find Redfield working in his woodshop. Redfield misunderstood Dechant's intentions and happily launched into a sales presentation. The show commenced with Redfield pulling hot, steam-heated quarter-sawn oak planks out of a bending box. With a dramatic amount of grunting and straining, he curved the hot oak around forms and clamped it into place, as he demonstrated for the strangers.

After that, Redfield pointed his visitors into his studio where he launched another impromptu sales pitch. The artist had three empty gilded frames, and he would pull 50 x 56-inch identically sized paintings, in quick succession, from a huge stack and drop them into the empty frames. He performed this quick frame exchange by hooking the

*Delaware Canal at New Hope*, Watercolor, 1938

toe of his slippers under the canvas and sliding the paintings into place. When Redfield began to realize that Miles wasn't there to buy paintings, he lost interest and the show was over.

Redfield was disappointed that he did not have a bona fide customer, and Miles was even more thwarted but for another reason: the artistic discussion he was hoping would ensue never materialized. Realistically, these sporadic meetings seldom lead to anything, but that did not lessen their importance. The two-hour drive to see Redfield was part of Dechant's quest for artistic validation. His frustration at this meeting was symptomatic of his dealings with the larger professional art world, where his intentions were misunderstood and he remained comparatively unknown and under-appreciated.

*On the Canal at New Hope,*
Oil, 1938

By the next year, Dechant's passion to expand his contacts in the art world lessened. The quest for artistic recognition seemed to lose significance, especially in light of the fact that at age 49, he was about to become a father again for the third time. He was excited. On April 5, 1939 Dorothy delivered her first baby, and Miles' last. They named their boy after Miles, but rather than make him a junior they gave him the middle name of Kachline, Dorothy's maiden name. For the father, babies were the sun and moon, all revolved in their orbit. With the arrival of Miles' first two children, his art life spun off course like a wayward comet; not to return for a very long time. It was logical that his art life would veer off course again, given the way so many aspects of his life repeated like a color motif.

Call it chromatic divergence, but with the birth of his new baby, Dechant did not take a painting hiatus. His passion for painting, if anything, seemed to increase. Perhaps it was a celebration of new life when he painted *The Lobachsville Bridge,* for it looks like the work of an artist reborn. Outwardly, the subject is a French version of that Pennsylvanian staple, the keystone bridge. But symbolically it is much more. Just as the church spire points heavenward, he found the same big movement in a humble little bridge. The arch and its reflection form a perfect circle, as if it is the earth itself, in partial eclipse. Resting on top of the world are the upward-intersecting lines of the bridge's peak; which point celestially, up beyond the earth's creatures, beyond its people, beyond its trees, to a heaven infinite, vast, and powder blue. *(Over)*

This striking combination of geometrically disparate shapes seemed to move him to re-invent his palette as well. He threw off years of Ed Clymer's color theory and his own use of "brilliant color and bold effects." He abandoned chromatic separation and allowed his palette to mellow with the same tonal separations of his French sojourn, almost but with more kick and vibrancy. Everywhere the muted shades repeat: blue sky and blue river, purple shadows and purple trees, tawny barn and tawny grass. No color appears alone, they all repeat. The underside of the arch and horseman, in deep black, provide contrast without disturbing the muted melody of tones. The beauty of this painting is not entirely contained in these details; it is a whole created with a singleness of purpose. In it, he hit his stride as a mature artist. From 1939 on, Dechant's skills were at the highest level of his career.

*The Lobachsville Bridge,*
Oil, 1939

Still celebrating their new baby and taking the chance to show him off
a little bit, the entire family of five traveled to Staten Island to stay with
Dorothy's "aunties." There was another reason behind this family out-
ing, the 1939 New York World's Fair. Miles took the lead as the family boarded a ferry bound for Manhattan and the fair in Flushing. Once
aboard the boat, he regaled them with tales of expositions past. He told
the older boys they were about to become witness to history. He was
well equipped to guide his family at this great exhibition, for his awe of
world fairs had roots in his childhood and the assassination of President

McKinley. By the time the ferry docked, the family's expectations were at fever pitch.

Miles was in his element from the moment he pushed through the turnstile. The fair was a feast for his eyes. He steered his boys away from the entertainment section, forcing them to see the wonders of science and great achievements in art and architecture. Their divergent interests found mutual agreement in the exhibition's highlights: Firestone with its miniature tire factory, Ford with its "Highway in the Sky," Chrysler with its "Frozen Forest." There Miles stood, beneath frozen palm trees, looking up at their dripping green ice fronds in amazement. Like a minister caught at a burlesque show, he was aghast at the gaudy, artificial beauties before him, yet found himself thrilled and delighted, unable to take his eyes away. He loved General Motor's Futurama, which held two people each in a string of moving chairs and encircled a diorama depicting life as it was 100 years in the past, in the present, and 20 years into the future. Designed by Norman Bel Geddes, the Futurama was a deco building, in a sea of deco buildings. Dechant, the sometime architect of deco buildings himself, was enthralled with the work of his better known contemporaries.

For the few wonderful hours he spent at the fair, Dechant embraced modernism in all its forms. Venturing onto the slippery slope of prediction, he told his sons, "Someday man will walk on the moon. I won't see it in my lifetime, but you boys probably will." He couldn't have known how short his lifetime was to be, but even as he spoke, he had difficulty catching his breath. Years of smoking had taken their toll, and even a short walk was exhausting for him. The strain of the fair was far beyond his capacity for exercise, but adrenaline had managed to carry him along. After three days of art pavilions and junk food, for which fairs are universally famous, he needed a break.

On August 6, the family drove home from the World's Fair. By the time their car pulled behind the house, the long shadows of late afternoon were fading into evening. Miles heard the phone ringing faintly as he approached the front door. As he fumbled with his keys, the phone kept ringing, echoing ominously in the dark, closed house. Finally reaching the phone, he answered and, as he listened, his family saw his face go ashen. A few moments later, he hung up, completely distraught. Everyone waited, wondering what happened. After a moment that hung for an eternity, his voice cracked, "My mother!"

Alone and shaken, he rushed out. By the time he got to his parents' house, his family had encircled his mother's bed in a deathwatch. Later that night, like a scene from a silent picture, the family doctor listened with his stethoscope and looked back to the family; solemnly he shook his head. Rebecca Dechant had died.

Miles' childhood home may have been full of people and furniture, but without his mother in it, the house seemed empty. The undertaker sent Rebecca's body back home the next day, and even the widowed husband seemed to brighten. Her open casket was placed in the living room, by the fireplace, at 535 North 5th Street. As people came in for the viewing, "Papa" sat alone next to "Mama" in a stiff-backed chair with his head bowed downward and his eyes closed most of the time. While family and friends silently glided in and out of the room, he remained a still, motionless figure forever locked into past memories. Separated by the length of the room and the gulf of mental decay, Miles watched his father. He knew the older man was incapable of remembering yesterday, and for a moment neither could he. He could only remember his mother's laugh, jolly and deep, "What will I do with my muddy boy?!"

While Miles was recovering from the loss of his mother, three weeks later he watched as his oldest son, Bill, geared up to leave for college. He had been accepted to Miles' alma mater, the University of Pennsylvania, to the pleasure of both father and son. But to their mutual displeasure, Miles could not afford tuition payments at the private Ivy League university. So Bill managed to locate a two-year school in Virginia, Bluefield College, where tuition was low and campus jobs could subsidize room and board. Bluefield was the answer to depression era finances, and Bill made ready to leave. Academically, it was a good choice.

*Winter Scene in Old Mt. Penn,* Oil, 1939

Miles decided to accompany his son to the train station and use the opportunity to give some last minute advice. His principle concern was the war, once more sweeping across Europe. Just days earlier, Hitler's armies had marched into Poland and set off World War II. The United States had promised to remain neutral, just as it had promised in 1917. Miles felt a sense of déjà vu and knew from experience that America would soon be at war again. As they drove to Harrisburg, he thought about the history of America's wars written in blood. Even the green valleys of Pennsylvania they were passing through had been home to the horrendous battles of the Civil War. He tried, as best he could, to warn his son of war's dangers. As they talked, Miles heard himself in the voice of his son, almost an echo over two decades. Miles' patriotism had tempered by time. After all the discussion about war, father and son arrived at Harrisburg and had to part. Dechant saved his final and most practical advice for last. He said, "I can't tell you not to smoke, but I can tell you not to drink. And don't smoke either!" Sending a child away from home for the first time, even for college, is a rite-of-passage. Miles returned home, worrying all the way about what the future would hold for his family.

Everywhere change was afoot. With the passing of his mother and decline of his father, the traditional Sunday family dinner was dismantling. Next year, on one of their last Sunday dinners together, Miles assumed his usual benevolent neutrality when Roosevelt's recent speech was discussed. After the German defeat of the French Army in June, Roosevelt had said "the hand that held the dagger has struck it into the back of its neighbor." The family discussion dissolved into an argument that mirrored the division of the American people, between those who would aid Europe and the isolationists who would have America stay out of the war. His provocateur brother, Fred, announced "The reason we need another good war is to cut down on all the excess population." His sisters, Mary and Sarah, and the other women jumped all over him. Miles, too, lost his calm and became angry as never before witnessed, almost shouting, "You can say that because you have three daughters, but I have sons!" This was followed by a stunned silence. The family was shocked to hear Miles raise his voice. This was a turning point in the lives of the Dechant family as well as the world: war was now a reality, not an abstraction, and a new unwelcome part of their lives. It was a moment that crystallized in the family memory, confirmation that change was in the air.

Even though change was inevitable, Miles still loved tradition and tried to maintain continuity. Larger forces were against him. Next year on September 16, 1940 the nation's first peacetime draft began. One of the first reserve officers to be recalled to duty was Fred Dechant, his 53-

year-old brother. Since the end of World War I, Fred had been an officer in the Navy Reserve, and he was called back to duty at the Brooklyn Navy Yard; by war's end he would be a captain. This was a hard loss for Miles because he was losing his brother as well as his business partner. The tradition of Miles' career within Wm. H. Dechant & Sons was at an end. He would have to run his own practice, and he dreaded the business aspects that involved. Underlying Miles' anxiety was the realization that if the Navy would haul an "old man" back, everyone else was fair game, too; he worried about his sons.

The following year Miles found a small bridge reminiscent to the one in Lobachsville. Again he put the human presence at the bridge peak.

*Oley Valley Bridge*, Watercolor, 1940

As a lone practitioner of architecture, he was barely scratching out a living. He was taking jobs a hundred miles away and commuting for on-site inspections. His only companion on these long drives was worry. He could worry about business, the war, and his children. He was a distracted driver on bad roads. In the late fall of 1940, Miles was designing a house for the Ford dealer near Lebanon and was driving to the job site. The sun was in his eyes, and as he squinted through windshield glare, he turned left ⌐ in front of a car he had not seen coming. The collision spun his Dodge around wildly, and before the car came to a rest, his left arm, his drawing arm, was broken in two places.

"Look at your father! Just look at him," Dorothy exclaimed when son Don came home from school. He saw his father, his arm in a cast, adhesive tape covering cuts and scratches, but talking about work. Miles ignored the cast and resumed his life. He never saw the cast as an impediment, but as an obstacle he could work around. With an early snowfall that year, cast or no cast, Miles was determined to paint. Don drove him to the Oley Valley in the patched-up Dodge. However, the crash had turned Miles from a dreaming passenger into a nervous participant. "Slow down! Watch out for that cow!" Both father and his son were relieved when he found a scene to paint. Not completely comfortable about painting with his right hand, nonetheless he set up his easel and appraised a sprawling log house with multiple generational additions. A red spring-house dominated the foreground, where icy jugs of milk sat in the spring water. But his eye kept being drawn back to the ancient log house and especially its roof, draped in dazzling white snow, like sugar icing on a ginger-bread house. Where does a one-armed painter make the first mark on paper? Miles knew that snowy roof could not be captured with paint. The only way to capture its brilliance was to avoid painting it entirely and allow the brilliance of the white drawing paper to represent the snow itself. Like a player of two-dimensional chess, if the artist wanted to end the composition with an unpainted area (the snow), that was where he would have to begin. Like writing a story in reverse, he radiated his brush strokes from where he would end. At its completion, the blank remained, just as planned; its rawness

*Log House Group,*
Watercolor, 1940

now boldly proclaimed a snowy roof. That day, in the snow, he proved one of art's absolute truths: the hand is secondary. Art is created, first and foremost, in the mind of the artist.

The painting, as good as it was, was the last Miles would create in the snowy outdoors. His health had deteriorated too far for the rigors of plein air painting in winter. That one day of exposure inflamed his annual winter cough, which lingered on well into the spring of 1941. Also lingering on was "Greyrock," an eclectic arts and crafts residence. Dechant had embarked on the well funded project with high hopes and designed a masterpiece along the lines of the gorgeous French chateaus he remembered so well. Alongside a small waterfall on Tulpehocken Creek, the site may have been serene, but the client was not. Scott

Althouse had made a fortune in the chemical business. He was a large, imposing man who always had the last word — it was his way or no way. His last home had burned down, and he was determined that the new one be impervious to fire. Miles' architectural drawings were scrutinized and changed by the client almost on a daily basis. Althouse would concoct elaborate scenarios whereby he found safety deficiencies in the plans. As was his wont, Dechant willingly fulfilled his client's wishes, but the struggle took its toil on his health, and there was no escape. The client was relentless in phoning the architect at the dinner hour. Always, when the phone rang, Miles felt obliged to answer as he knew it would be Althouse. As his dinner turned from warm to cold, Althouse would talk on and on, demanding one change after another. Hanging up the receiver, Miles would fume, "There's just no way to ever satisfy that man."

Compounding Dechant's client frustrations were worries about his father's health. As his difficult year wore on, his beloved father entered the last stages of senility. Although his father was physically present, he was mentally absent. Seeing him this way was both disturbing and haunting to Miles. It had even been a long time since his father worked himself into his once daily ritual of agitated confusion entitled "Looking for Mama." This oft-repeated scenario would see William throwing the house into disorder in a futile search for his deceased wife. Now he sat and seldom spoke: the transition from dynamic patriarch to dying parent was difficult to watch.

"There is a true relationship existing between father and son, tied by God's love." That was a message William long ago had written his son. That father-son bond would never unravel, but after 90 years of life, William's fire was burning out. Shortly after his beloved wife's death, William was moved to his daughter Sarah's home in Dallas, Pennsylvania — although his mind remained home in Reading. On October 7, 1941 twilight's last train hissed by the side porch once again, building steam and pushing out cumulous clouds of black soot. The engineer yanked on the whistle cord, and the hollow roar echoed through his father's dreams one last time. Then the noise, so full only moments before, evaporated, steaming headlong for the open silver rails.

Though he had not been able to communicate with his father for years, Miles was shaken by his death. Dechant lost more than his father: he lost his best friend, his business partner, his most trusted advisor, and the man he respected most in the entire world. As Miles did his best to recover and calm his nerves, World War II was escalating. On Dec. 7, 1941 radio stations began interrupting their programs with this startling announcement: "We bring you a special bulletin. At 7:58 this morning Japanese planes attacked Pearl Harbor." Dechant went home and sat by the radio as excited newscasters told of the events of a day which, in President Roosevelt's words, would "live in infamy." These announcements made him sick with worry as two of his boys were now draft age and in college. He counted the days until his boys would come home for Christmas. As days of waiting passed, he heard little good news. Congress declared war on Japan, and then Germany declared war on the United States.

Finally, a few days before Christmas, Bill and Don came home from college. They were shocked to see how much their father had aged. He would head upstairs to get something, but was unable to climb more than a step or two without stopping to rest. His new business cards had been left haphazardly on the entryway table. They read: Announcing the Removal of the Offices of Miles B. Dechant, Architect, to 250 Friedensburg Road. He had not mentioned anything to the boys previously, but finances were forcing him to close his business office. This signaled rock bottom for Miles; he had always maintained a first class professional office in downtown Reading, and now he soon would be relegated to working from home. When he came back downstairs, he mentioned nothing of the cards, and his whole family gathered around the RCA radio. In addition to the destruction in Hawaii, Wake Island, a U. S. base in the central Pacific, also was being attacked by the Japanese. Miles listened to the radio broadcast late into the night. In his whole life, he had never been to a tropical island or even seen the Pacific Ocean. The dangers he heard about were in places he could only imagine.

By Christmas Eve, his spirits had brightened. Watching his wife and children decorate the Christmas tree, he sat down and said, "I'm going to read a little." Determined to uphold the traditions he found dear, he read aloud from "The Night Before Christmas" and "A Christmas Carol." Sometime before the ghost of Christmas Future made his appearance, Miles' voice trailed off into silence, and his family tiptoed off to bed. The artist, asleep in his chair, had weathered a terrible year. His father's death, difficult clients, war worries, but most of all, failing health, had all conspired to eviscerate his creativity.

After Christmas was celebrated, Dechant thought maybe he should begin a new painting. As he looked through his painting supplies, he saw everything had become neglected. Paint had dried in the tubes, he had eight shades of green, no blue whatsoever, little paper, and no canvas. Despite an ache in his chest and shortness of breath, he wanted to re-stock what he needed. He could not buy quality supplies in Reading; he preferred an art store called F.W. Weber in Philadelphia. His son, Bill, drove him there, and he remembers his dad could barely walk from the curb on Chestnut Street to the store, stopping every few feet to catch his breath. Once in the store he bought 15 tubes of paint, a thick pad of watercolor paper, and most important, he said, a big square canvas.

Dechant had his son bring the big canvas up to his second floor studio. It was an ambitious size, and Miles felt unwell. But he began to work, as if under a premonition. He poked the fresh, white canvas and felt its resiliency spring back against his fingers. There was nothing like a fresh tube of paint to squeeze out, so buttery and fat when it was brand new; and as he scooped his flat bristle brush into the mountain of snowy white paint his palette held, he paused. He stared at his reference, a pencil sketch he had made in the fall. Of it, he said simply, "I always thought it would be a good painting." He wanted to make it great, and the importance of that weighed on the freedom of his brush from his first stroke.

As the days wore on, the indoor painting became more narrative than impressionistic. The composition was flat; the proportions strange. The themes were familiar, farmhouse and river. In the lower right he painted the symbol, the talisman and mascot of his artistic life, the row boat. There the little boat floats, ominously empty. The boatsman had stopped navigating life's river, and stepped ashore. Dechant struggled with the story he wanted to tell and how to tell it. He usually painted quickly and lightly; dabbing colors here and there with the surety of a virtuoso pianist playing a familiar piece. This one was entirely different. He was hesitant. He would put on a few strokes and then constantly step back and study it. He abandoned color harmonies, choosing to paint in small patches of color, which clashed as if they had been plucked at random from a whirling vortex of human suffering. Pale reds and yellow greens mixed together like strident acids. These were not the accurate colors of dying leaves; they were more the accurate colors of a dying mind. Miles jabbed away at the canvas.

"Dad, it's time to go," his sons interrupted his painting. Miles pulled the pocket watch from his vest and looked at it. His boys were ready to return to college, but he was not ready to take them to the train station. He wanted to give them some last message, but he had not found the words, yet. Nothing came to mind, not even on the train platform.

His son, Don, remembers the evening:

> We were standing on the platform, and I was getting cold. Dad was there, and I think now, he realized he wouldn't see us again. I didn't have that perception then, I was cold, and I said, 'I'm going to go get in the train. It's going to leave in 10 minutes, anyway.' So I said good-bye to Dad and I got in the train. Bill stayed with him.

Bill recalls:

> I stayed because I had a feeling that maybe Dad wanted to tell me something. He seemed to mind the separation more than usual.

In those few fleeting minutes, Miles didn't say anything Bill can remember. But when the final whistle blew, his father's face became etched in memory, "Dad had tears in his eyes." Blinking them away, Miles watched the train pull away as if in slow motion. He would never see his two older sons again.

Dechant painted at least a little bit every day for the rest of the week trying to finish the big, square canvas. While he painted, disparate images flashed through his mind: he saw people and places he had long ago forgotten. He had trouble concentrating and nothing looked right. Unsettled, he decided he must finish the painting that night. Miles worked into the wee hours of the morning, still unsatisfied. But he was too tired to go on; it was done. He signed it haphazardly, left off the date, turned and walked down the hall. As a final summation of all he learned, and felt and lived, the painting was a disappointment for Miles. It was, and still is, impossible to summate all one's life on command. It may happen a few times in the life of an artist, like a hole in one for a golfer, and it probably is not going to happen on the last swing at it. As a painting, Miles sliced the ball way high and right, and he knew it. It is not a fair impression of the Pennsylvania countryside, but as an impression of a dying mind, it is a masterpiece. In its flaws, it expresses life's difficulties and joys — like the visual equivalent of a poet's last words. (*Opposite*)

The painting's completion left Miles exhausted. He could barely pull himself from bed in the morning. When he did, he felt his chest tighten. Mechanically he drove to his nearly vacant office. There, surrounded by moving boxes, he sat behind the drafting board. Leaning over to draw, a shooting pain went through his chest. He took some aspirin and tried to relax. By mid afternoon the pain was worse. He left his work and went to the office of Dr. Miller. The folksy family doctor listened with his stethoscope; then looked up at Miles' ashen face. In a surprised voice he said, "You're having a mild heart attack." Dechant struggled to hold on to his composure, "That's pretty serious, isn't it?" Dr. Miller shook his head and spoke reassuringly, "Don't worry about it, Miles. Just last week, I had one, too. You need to go home and lie on the couch."

Miles reclined in a chair at home, but by then his chest was in excruciating pain. Frantically, Dorothy called the doctor out to the house. In

In his last weeks, Miles transformed his physical deterioration into a work of disturbing beauty. He was a true believer in the transformative power of art. The many paintings Miles did in his life stand as a testament to his belief in art, and they have remained beautiful in the more than half century since his death. They stand in sharp contrast to a life that was beautiful but too brief.

*Season Change*, Oil, 1942

agitated, nervous pain, Miles joked with him. Dr. Miller said, "Miles, you have a good sense of humor; you'd laugh on your deathbed." Dorothy saw the doctor out the door and was going upstairs on an errand, when she heard a loud thud. She came running back to find that Miles had fallen, trying to raise himself. He was on the floor, and Dorothy could not move him. She ran for a neighbor, and together they dragged him back up on the couch, still breathing but unconscious. He lay once more on his favorite couch, his many paintings looking down upon him. Miles looked back at them no more on that pale January evening. With his eyes tightly shut, he journeyed along a golden country lane towards a destination infinitely more picturesque.

*This old chateau was as silent as the bodies of those who lived in it once upon a time, but who live no more. The wind through the gigantic and specter-like trees, made melancholy music as it came and went. The cheerful laughter of those who so joyously built and constructed this building is no longer heard. But their hearts and thoughts, embodied in stone, stand here before us.*

*Miles Boyer Dechant*
*France ~ August 20, 1918.*

117

Today Miles Dechant is remembered mainly by family, on whose walls his paintings age ever so quietly.                                                      *The Color of the Day*, Watercolor,  1933

118

# ACKNOWLEDGMENTS

It would be impossible to adequately thank all the people who helped with this undertaking. Please understand that for each deed of assistance I cite there were probably ten more. Here then, in non-alphabetical order, are the people to whom I am particularly indebted.

Shelley Sjoberg Dechant of Los Angeles, California. My wife, my muse, to whom I dedicate my work. She was my constant consultant and first advisor. Shelley challenged and encouraged me to do my best work.

Lois and Donald H. Dechant of La Jolla, California, my parents. My mother helped me edit the biography from first draft to final revision, and my father was and is my inspiration. The heart of the book is the story of my grandfather, as remembered by my father and his brother William. Without their memories, there would have been no story.

June and William G. Dechant of Brevard, North Carolina. They took two weeks helping me photograph paintings in North Carolina. My father joined us there and Bill drove the three of us to Reading, Pennsylvania for my one week introduction to the city. Their generosity was overwhelming.

Betty and Miles Kachline Dechant of Reading, Pennsylvania. Without their involvement the biography would have been much poorer. He provided photography and supplied MBD's written biographical material: the high school speech, articles, correspondence and hand written letters from World War I. Betty transcribed the letters from France and helped xerox many documents. Their kindness and cooperation are most appreciated.

Dorothy Kachline Dechant (Deceased) of Reading, Pennsylvania. I drew from her family genealogy, circa 1970.

My brothers and sisters-in-law: Linda and Donald J. Dechant, and Kerri and Stephenson Miles Dechant of San Diego, California. Offered advice, support, and encouragement.

My cousins in North Carolina: Judi Dechant Allen and the late Louis Allen, Lake Junaluska; Kay and Thomas F. Dechant, and Kim and William Miles Dechant, all of Asheville. They allowed me to photograph their collections and were most gracious. William permitted me to use some thoughts from his architectural graduate thesis on our grandfather MBD.

Peggy Schultz (widow of William D. Schultz) of Santa Monica, California and her daughter and son-in-law, Susan and Bob Karp of Pacific Palisades, California. Shared memories of Mary Dechant Schultz (MBD's sister), and were most generous.

Kitty and Bill Filling of Millersville, and Gwen and John Hauck of Carlisle, Pennsylvania. They welcomed us and let me photograph their paintings (Kitty and John are the children of MBD's sister Sarah).

Phyllis and Edwin Garvin Miller of Lancaster, Pennsylvania. For their hospitality and help.

Brian H. Peterson and Erika Jaeger Smith of the James A. Michener Museum in Bucks County, Pennsylvania. Generously allowed my interview. I borrowed heavily from their ideas about Pennsylvania impressionism.

Deborah Winkler at The Reading Public Museum. Made their collection available for photography.

Harold Yoder of the Berks County Historical Society. Allowed me to photograph their collection.

P.J. Castellaneta of Los Angeles, James Slocum of South Pasadena, and Steve Masias of Tujunga, California. All gave me thoughtful insights on the rough manuscript.

Bart Ryckbosch, Archivist at The Art Institute of Chicago.

Cheryl Leibold, Archivist at the Pennsylvania Academy of the Fine Arts.

Martin Hackett, Archivist at the University of Pennsylvania.

Barry Brooks of Studio City, California. My talented book designer. His experience was invaluable as he guided the project to completion.

# Selected Bibliography

## Books

Austrian, Geoffrey D. *Ben Austrian, Artist*. Laurys Station, Pennsylvania: Garrigues House, Publishers, 1997

Bush, George S. *The Genius Belt: The Story of the Arts in Bucks County, Pennsylvania*. Doylestown , Pennsylvania: James A. Michener Art Museum in association with the Pennsylvania State University Press, 1996.

Bayer, Patricia. *Art Deco Architecture: design, decoration, and detail for the twenties and thirties*. New York: Harry N. Abrams Publishers, 1992.

Falk, Peter Hastings ed., *Who Was Who in American Art*. Madison, Connecticut: Sound View Press, 1999.

Folk, Thomas C. *The Pennsylvania Impressionists*. Cranbury, New Jersey: Associated University Presses, 1997.

McGlauflin, Alice Coe, ed. *Who's Who in American Art, Volume II, 1938-1939*. Washington D.C., USA: The American Federation of Arts, 1937.

Peterson, Brian H. *Intimate Vistas: The Poetic Landscapes of William Langson Lathrop*. Bucks County, Pennsylvania: James A. Michener Art Museum, 1999.

Siskind, Aaron. *Bucks County: Photographs of Early Architecture*. New York: Horizon Press, 1974.

Swank, Scott T. *Arts of the Pennsylvania Germans*. New York, New York; W.W. Norton & Company, Inc. 1983

Turner, Elizabeth Hutton. *American Artists in Paris, 1919-1929*. Ann Arbor, Michigan: UMI Research Press, 1988.

Wallace, Robert. *The World of Van Gogh 1853-1890*. Alexandria, Virginia: Time-Life Books, 1977.

Weiser, C.Z., D.D. *A Monograph of The New Goschenhoppen and Great Swamp Reformed Charge, 1731-1881*. Reading, Pennsylvania: Daniel Miller, Printer, 1882.

## Periodicals

Borelli, Joelyn, "Miles Boyer Dechant." *The Historical Review of Berks County*. Summer 1957.

Dechant, Miles Boyer A.I.A. "Eight Houses for the Hampden Heights Development Company, Reading, Pennsylvania." *American Architect*, September 20, 1928.

Dechant, Miles Boyer A.I.A. "Music for Reading, Pa." *Architectural Concrete*, Volume 5, Number 4.

Dechant, Miles Boyer A.I.A. "The Boyer Towne Inn at the Towne Cross Roads." *Unidentified clipping*.

Dunkelberger, James E. "Berks County Court Houses." *The Historical Review of Berks County*. October-December 1951.

Flippen, Paula M. "Miles B. Dechant." *The Historical Review of Berks County*. Spring 1980.

Fryer, Benjamin A. "Court House Result of 20 Years' Clamor." *Reading Times*. July 12, 1932.

McClellan, Mabel K. "The Story of Reading's Second Boys' High School." *The Historical Review of Berks County*. Spring 1962.

Phillips, Raymond J. "The Reading Socialists In Retrospect." *The Historical Review of Berks County*. Summer 1965.

# Photography Credits

Copyright © 2002 by Miles K. Dechant: all rights reserved on pages 6, 62, 65, 80, 90, 93, 117 • *The Reading Eagle* page 69 • Donald H. Dechant page 72 • Otherwise by author or unknown photographers.

# Colophon

The text for this book was set in a digitized version of the typeface Goudy. The American designer, Frederic W. Goudy (1865-1947) based this type on traditional Roman letters. First released in 1915, its graceful, freehand drawn letterforms made it an instant classic and captured some feeling of that period.

Printed on 100 pound Meade Matte Book - Archival Paper ~ Printed by Primary Color  ~  Los Angeles, California, USA

Designed by Barry Brooks